SPEAKING TO THE HEART

SPEAKING TO THE HEART

Favourite Poems
chosen and introduced by

Sister Wendy Beckett

CONSTABLE · LONDON

Constable & Robinson Ltd
3 The Lanchesters
162 Fulham Palace Road
London W6 9ER
www.constablerobinson.com

First published in the UK by Constable,
an imprint of Constable & Robinson Ltd 2006

A copy of the British Library Cataloguing in
Publication Data is available from the British Library

ISBN-13: 978-1-84529-465-6
ISBN-10: 1-84529-465-3

Printed and bound in the EU

3 5 7 9 10 8 6 4

CONTENTS

✦ ✦ ✦

Introduction by ... Wendy Barker

POEMS

WOMEN

CONTENTS

————❖❖❖————

CONTENTS

A LIGHTER SPIRIT

THE HEAVY HEART

CONTENTS

COURAGE

SORROW

CONTENTS

FAITH

HOPE

CONTENTS

LOVE

PRAYER

INTRODUCTION

❖ ❖ ❖

Mᴷ PUBLISHER, who is an inventive man, suggested that I group the poems in this anthology under the various vices and virtues. I rather took to this idea. Especially when it came to the vices, I have long thought that the catechism list of seven is inadequate. There seems to me only one all-consuming monster of a vice and that is pride. Pride sees itself as so completely the centre that all else is subordinate to its needs: pride is the world, other people, the planets. Others are to be raged at when they thwart my desires (anger); their bodies offer me pleasure (lust); it is for me to eat as much and as well as I choose regardless of the world's hunger (gluttony); the possessions and achievements and even the happiness of other people is mine by right and I rage at the injustice of not possessing it (envy and covetousness). The only vice that has a faint claim to its own status is perhaps sloth, but even then the characteristic of sloth is a complete abdication of all responsibility except for my own sole welfare.

The name I prefer for this hideous and distorted quality is not pride but irreverence, or, if you like, disrespect. Reverence gives to every person and each object its own unique importance. It will never override, it will never

1

subordinate, it can see the beauty of all that *is*, without a desire to seize it in one's own clammy hands. But in the catechism list, reverence does not appear under the virtues.

I could understand why I could not find poetry to illustrate the hideous reality of the vices. What is dark and dead and repulsive is not likely to give rise to poetry. What then of the virtues? Here again, I looked glumly at the list. I could find poems about faith, hope and charity, but all too often they were nauseatingly pious verse rather than poetry and when I looked at the four cardinal virtues – prudence, justice, fortitude and temperance – my heart sank still lower. Fortitude perhaps had possibilities; courage has brought forth much magnificent poetry; but prudence? Justice? Still less poor strait-laced temperance. Who has been sufficiently gifted to hymn them? I decided my publisher was too inventive for his own good and started at the other end.

I began to draw from my memory and from my stacks of poetry anthologies and from poems cut out of magazines and newspapers the poetry that I really loved. I went back to lines I have known for almost seventy years as well as those that have filled me with delight when I came across them in literary magazines. Of course, I then amassed far too many, but even exercising the most stringent economy I was left with a goodly collection of poetry that was dear to me. At first, the only prevalent emotion that I could identify was longing (I have a fatal weakness for Housman and Hardy) and wonder. Yet as I went through the poems more carefully, I found to my astonishment that in actual fact I had come pretty close, at least as regards the virtues, to my original quest.

These are not the virtues in their religious sense, or at least not necessarily so. What we have here is a spiritual sense, something far wider and more elemental. There is religious poetry, with its defining religious vocabulary, but not much of it here. Just as I have always felt the essence of great painting was its spirituality, and that this applies as much to Degas's ballet dancers as it does to Fra Angelico's virgins, so is it true of poetry. If the poet is not speaking from his own emotional depths to our own sense of freedom and strength of spirit, then this is not poetry to which I am attracted.

There are poems here that could certainly be grouped under the headings of Faith, Hope and Love; Fortitude or Courage also. Longing and Wonder, which are so obviously present in many poems, are surely both virtues. Sorrow is a perennial poetic theme. The light-heartedness that so attracts us in some poetry can be counter-balanced with that dark- or heavy-heartedness that is the sole remaining trace from my original search for poems about vice.

You will notice that all the poems I have chosen speak directly to the heart. I like abstruse poetry too (the ineffable inexplicabilities of Empson, let us say), but since one cannot include everything I have chosen those that thrust themselves powerfully upon my emotions. Some of these poems speak to the heart with elegance and a certain distance. Technically, 'Lycidas' is too long for this anthology, yet it exemplifies supremely all that matters most to me in poetry. Ezra Pound specified – and who better to dictate a poetical ethos – that poetry does not consist of ideas but of words; the ideas must be there, of course, and emotion becomes sentimentality if it is not enhanced with intellectual content, but it is above all the music of the actual words that carries the power of a poem. Of all definitions of poetry, the one that appeals to me most is that it is the most economical use of words. It is the task of the poet not only to find the best words, the true words, but to set them in metrical order so that the very movement of the verse amplifies the meaning, and that one note calls forth another until every word in every line is contributing to the poetic symphony. Referring back to 'Lycidas', I think we have here the most perfect example of poetic music in our language. The poem moves through great fields of emotional involvement but always with such a richly singing tone that Milton's excoriation of the false shepherds, the religious ministry of the seventeenth century, is as wonderful to the ear as his exhortation of the beautiful friend whose death he is lamenting. It seems to me that, in lesser compass, every poem in this anthology does something similar – or attempts with fair success to achieve that goal.

With painting I have found that people sometimes need support, but once launched they are perfectly capable of responding to a work of art. Poetry, though, does not seem to need a midwife with the same urgency. There are, of course, difficult poems, often of superlative and mind-expanding beauty, but by and large most poems give up their secret sweetly and easily. If we are willing to listen not only to what they say, but how they say it, they speak very clearly and directly to us, heart to heart.

Even if you knew no English, I think listening to these poems would stir your emotions, but those who are privileged to speak and understand our language can be moved at many levels. Even the light-hearted poems have an emotional significance, however gaily and sweetly they may treat it. What I so value here is that in every case, or so it seems to me, the significance does not have to be puzzled out, but comes to us with an immediacy and a power that are the ultimate proof of what poetry can be. Every poem here is dear to me. Dear reader, I hope they may become dear to you as well.

Sister Wendy Beckett

Quidenham,
Norfolk, England
March 2006

LONGING

❖❖❖

TO LONG AFTER, to reach out for, to look back with an intense regret: these are emotions that we all experience. The academic word for this perpetual sense of unfulfilment is 'nostalgia', but to me it seems overly confining with its suggestions of the pining after childhood, or homesickness. Yet we are also homesick if we think of our home as not truly of this world but, as we read in St Paul, our homeland in heaven. Even the most adamant atheist will admit to feeling not totally at home in this beautiful world of ours. Beauty catches us at the throat with its overwhelming implications of purity and grace that we can never possess. We are always pulled outward and upward, and poetry that both celebrates and mourns the state of incompleteness is more precious to me than I had suspected before I started collecting poems for this anthology.

Ode on a Grecian Urn

John Keats 1795–1821

KEATS is pre-eminently the poet of longing. He was young, poor and unsuccessful (or so the scornful critics of the literary journals of his time led him to believe). Above all, he knew only too well, being a medical student and having nursed his brother Tom through a painful illness and a tubercular death, that his own tuberculosis would make it impossible for him to achieve any of his ambitions. He could never marry his darling Fanny Brawne, he could never write the poetry of which he dreamed. All too swiftly he would die, gasping for breath and coughing up blood. He told his friend Thomas Southern, who looked after him, to write on his tomb: 'Here lies one whose name was writ in water'.

Keats is the touchstone of whether we can respond to poetry. He has an awareness of the beauty of words and their music that takes us out of ourselves into the nostalgic world that he describes. Here, when he is describing the pictures on a Grecian urn, we feel the intensity of his longing to live in a world that is frozen in space. In the ideal world of the urn the characters are always happy, and will never pass through time into unhappiness. By his own deep awareness of the ravages of time and his effortless use of the words that take us into the emotion, Keats truly speaks to the heart.

Thou still unravished bride of quietness,
　Thou foster-child of Silence and slow Time,
Sylvan historian, who canst thus express
　A flowery tale more sweetly than our rhyme:
What leaf-fringed legend haunts about thy shape
　Of deities or mortals, or of both,
　　In Tempe or the dales of Arcady?
　What men or gods are these? What maidens loth?
What mad pursuit? What struggle to escape?
　　What pipes and timbrels? What wild ecstasy?

Heard melodies are sweet, but those unheard
　Are sweeter; therefore, ye soft pipes, play on;
Not to the sensual ear, but, more endeared,
　Pipe to the spirit ditties of no tone:
Fair youth, beneath the trees, thou canst not leave
　Thy song, nor ever can those trees be bare;
　　Bold Lover, never, never canst thou kiss,
Though winning near the goal – yet, do not grieve;
　She cannot fade, though thou hast not thy bliss,
　　For ever wilt thou love, and she be fair!

Ah, happy, happy boughs! that cannot shed
　Your leaves, nor ever bid the Spring adieu;
And, happy melodist, unwearièd,
　For ever piping songs for ever new;
More happy love! more happy, happy love!
　For ever warm and still to be enjoyed,
　　For ever panting and for ever young;

9

All breathing human passion far above,
That leaves a heart high-sorrowful and cloyed,
A burning forehead, and a parching tongue.

Who are these coming to the sacrifice?
To what green altar, O mysterious priest,
Lead'st thou that heifer lowing at the skies,
And all her silken flanks with garlands drest?
What little town by river or sea-shore,
Or mountain-built with peaceful citadel,
Is emptied of this folk, this pious morn?
And, little town, thy streets for evermore
Will silent be; and not a soul to tell
Why thou art desolate, can e'er return.

O Attic shape! Fair attitude! with brede
Of marble men and maidens overwrought,
With forest branches and the trodden weed;
Thou, silent form! dost tease us out of thought
As doth eternity. Cold Pastoral!
When old age shall this generation waste,
Thou shalt remain, in midst of other woe
Than ours, a friend to man, to whom thou sayst,
'Beauty is truth, truth beauty, – that is all
Ye know on earth, and all ye need to know.'

Piano

D. H. Lawrence 1885–1930

ONCE YOU grow up you can never again be part of your mother's personal 'music'. You will notice that D. H. Lawrence does not want to experience this longing – 'in spite of myself, the insidious mastery of song betrays me back'. He wants to stay the fully armoured adult, but music takes him back into that world with 'winter outside'. He wants that great sense of safety and security that you have, if you are fortunate, as a child. If you read this with care, it is obvious it is a major poem, not just a sentimental magazine piece, as casual readers have sometimes believed. All sentimentality is based on a truth which has been downgraded, but the truth in this poem is fresh and original.

Softly, in the dusk, a woman is singing to me;
Taking me back down the vista of years, till I see
A child sitting under the piano, in the boom of the
     tingling strings
And pressing the small, poised feet of a mother who
     smiles as she sings.

In spite of myself, the insidious mastery of song
Betrays me back, till the heart of me weeps to belong
To the old Sunday evenings at home, with winter
     outside
And hymns in the cosy parlour, the tinkling piano our
     guide.

So now it is vain for the singer to burst into clamour
With the great black piano appassionato. The
    glamour
Of childish days is upon me, my manhood is cast
Down in the flood of remembrance, I weep like a
    child for the past.

———— ❖❖❖ ————

Chanson Innocente

e. e. cummings 1894–1962

THERE IS ALWAYS an imaginary element in nostalgia because the world to which we long to return is partly non-existent. In e.e.cummings's imaginary world of childhood – an idyllic world that is gone for ever – the man who sells balloons is a goat-footed Pan, but in the adult world, Pan is a tricksy and tainted semi-divinity. Cummings yearns back towards a time when he and his friends were still innocent, although the uncomplicated happiness of which he sings was in reality far more complex and difficult.

      in Just-
      spring   when the world is mud-
      luscious the little
      lame balloonman

whistles   far   and wee

and eddieandbill come
running from marbles and
piracies and it's
spring

 when the world is puddle-wonderful

the queer
old balloonman whistles
far   and   wee
and bettyandisbel come dancing
from hop-scotch and jump-rope and

it's
spring
and
   the
        goat-footed
balloonMan   whistles
far
and
wee

The Wild Swans at Coole

W. B. Yeats 1865–1939

THE SENSE OF CHILL silence and beauty is something Yeats communicates with poignancy and passion. This is the poem among all his masterpieces which I love best, both for its simplicity and its power.

> The trees are in their autumn beauty,
> The woodland paths are dry,
> Under the October twilight the water
> Mirrors a still sky;
> Upon the brimming water among the stones
> Are nine-and-fifty swans.
>
> The nineteenth autumn has come upon me
> Since I first made my count;
> I saw, before I had well finished,
> All suddenly mount
> And scatter wheeling in great broken rings
> Upon their clamorous wings.
>
> I have looked upon those brilliant creatures,
> And now my heart is sore.
> All's changed since I, hearing at twilight,
> The first time on this shore,
> The bell-beat of their wings above my head,
> Trod with a lighter tread.

Unwearied still, lover by lover,
They paddle in the cold
Companionable streams or climb the air;
Their hearts have not grown old;
Passion or conquest, wander where they will,
Attend upon them still.

But now they drift on the still water,
Mysterious, beautiful;
Among what rushes will they build,
By what lake's edge or pool
Delight men's eyes when I awake some day
To find they have flown away?

——— ❖❖❖ ———

Written in Northampton County Asylum
John Clare 1793–1864

TO MY SHAME it has taken me a long time to warm to
John Clare (I think what held me back was his use of
language, which I found, initially, too plebeian). But here
it is the very ordinariness of his words that make the sen-
timent so moving. We are drawn to set the painful humil-
ity of the writer against the humiliating constrictions of
his actual situation. Not only to be confined to an asylum,
but to labour all one's life against mental infirmity, makes
all that he writes heroic.

I am! yet what I am who cares, or knows?
   My friends forsake me like a memory lost.
I am the self-consumer of my woes;
   They rise and vanish, an oblivious host,
Shadows of life, whose very soul is lost.
And yet I am – I live – though I am tossed

Into nothingness of scorn and noise,
   Into the living sea of waking dream,
Where there is neither sense of life, nor joys,
   But the huge shipwreck of my own esteem
And all that's dear. Even those I loved the best
Are strange – nay, they are stranger than the rest.

I long for scenes where man has never trod –
   For scenes where woman never smiled or wept –
There to abide with my Creator, God,
   And sleep as I in childhood sweetly slept,
Full of high thoughts, unborn. So, let me lie –
The grass below; above, the vaulted sky.

'Into my heart an air that kills'
A. E. Housman 1859–1936

As a person imprisoned in a carapace of scholarly austerity and, one gathers, deeply unlikeable, Housman's vulnerability comes across in his poetry. One sometimes finds that the qualities an artist or a poet has excluded from his life are the very qualities to be found in his work: companionship, warmth and sharing are all there.

'Into my heart an air that kills' sums up the longing that haunts all art; the happiness has gone and even being aware of past happiness is painful. This is a much more dramatic and agonized statement of the same theme that e. e. cummings wrote about in 'Chanson Innocente'.

> Into my heart an air that kills
>   From yon far country blows:
> What are those blue remembered hills,
>   What spires, what farms are those?
>
> That is the land of lost content,
>   I see it shining plain,
> The happy highways where I went
>   And cannot come again.

Utopia

Wislawa Szymborska b. 1923

*Translated by Stanislaw Baranczak
and Clare Cavanagh*

THIS IS AN ironic view of what we long for life to be: controllable and sensible and quite unlike the way it really is. Wislawa Szymborska is Polish and won the Nobel Prize for Literature in 1996.

Island where all becomes clear.

Solid ground beneath your feet.

The only roads are those that offer access.

Bushes bend beneath the weight of proofs.

The Tree of Valid Supposition grows here
with branches disentangled since time immemorial.

The Tree of Understanding, dazzlingly straight and
    simple,
sprouts by the spring called Now I Get It.

The thicker the woods, the vaster the vista:
the Valley of Obviously.

If any doubts arise, the wind dispels them instantly.

Echoes stir unsummoned
and eagerly explain all the secrets of the worlds.

On the right a cave where Meaning lies.

On the left the Lake of Deep Conviction.
Truth breaks from the bottom and bobs to the
    surface.

Unshakable Confidence towers over the valley.
Its peak offers an excellent view of the Essence of
    Things.

For all its charms, the island is uninhabited,
and the faint footprints scattered on its beaches
turn without exception to the sea.

As if all you can do here is leave
and plunge, never to return, into the depths.

Into unfathomable life.

The Solitary Reaper

William Wordsworth 1770–1850

IN DOROTHY WORDSWORTH'S journals she speaks about the incident described in this poem. We know that she and William passed a girl singing in the fields and in this poem the poet remembers that girl's solitary song and the feelings it aroused in him. The plaintive notes of Celtic music always conjure a sense of longing, a sense of the inevitable disappointments of life and of its essential sadness. There is a fundamental lack of fulfilment from which we all suffer, yet paradoxically we all listen to poignant music that arouses our desire for what is beyond our reach. Wordsworth heard that music and stresses that even when we have passed beyond the singer, the music remains in the heart.

> Behold her, single in the field,
> Yon solitary Highland Lass!
> Reaping and singing by herself;
> Stop here, or gently pass!
> Alone she cuts and binds the grain,
> And sings a melancholy strain;
> O listen! for the Vale profound
> Is overflowing with the sound.
>
> No Nightingale did ever chaunt
> More welcome notes to weary bands
> Of travellers in some shady haunt,

Among Arabian sands:
A voice so thrilling ne'er was heard
In spring-time from the Cuckoo-bird,
Breaking the silence of the seas
Among the farthest Hebrides.

Will no one tell me what she sings? –
Perhaps the plaintive numbers flow
For old, unhappy, far-off things,
And battles long ago:
Or is it some more humble lay,
Familiar matter of today?
Some natural sorrow, loss, or pain,
That has been, and may be again?

Whate'er the theme, the Maiden sang
As if her song could have no ending;
I saw her singing at her work,
And o'er the sickle bending: –
I listened, motionless and still:
And, as I mounted up the hill,
The music in my heart I bore,
Long after it was heard no more.

'They are all gone into the world of light'

Henry Vaughan 1621–95

IF WE HAVE true faith, we believe that those we have loved and lost – people and animals – have moved into the 'world of light' and we long to follow them. This poem could have been entitled 'Prayer': it is so specific in its unspoken plea to become part of that liberating eternity that allows us to escape from the constrictions of time.

They are all gone into the world of light!
    And I alone sit lingring here;
Their very memory is fair and bright,
    And my sad thoughts doth clear.

It glows and glitters in my cloudy brest
    Like stars upon some gloomy grove,
Or those faint beams in which this hill is drest,
      After the Sun's remove.

I see them walking in an Air of glory,
    Whose light doth trample on my days:
My days, which are at best but dull and hoary,
      Meer glimering and decays.

O holy hope! and high humility,
    High as the Heavens above!
These are your walks, and you have shew'd them me
      To kindle my cold love.

Dear, beauteous death! the Jewel of the Just,
   Shining no where, but in the dark;
What mysteries do lie beyond thy dust;
     Could man outlook that mark!

He that hath found some fledg'd bird's nest,
     may know
   At first sight, if the bird be flown;
But what fair Well, or Grove he sings in now,
     That is to him unknown.

And yet, as Angels in some brighter dreams
   Call to the soul, when man doth sleep:
So some strange thoughts transcend our
     wonted theams,
     And into glory peep.

If a star were confin'd into a Tomb
   Her captive flames must needs burn there;
But when the hand that lockt her up, gives room,
     She'll shine through all the sphære.

O Father of eternal life, and all
   Created glories under thee!
Resume thy spirit from this world of thrall
     Into true liberty.

Either disperse these mists, which blot and fill
   My perspective (still) as they pass,
Or else remove me hence unto that hill
     Where I shall need no glass.

WONDER

WE ENVY CHILDREN their capacity for wonder. I think one of the greatest qualities of poetry is that it can elevate us into the state of wonder experienced by the poet. The child knows wonder because it has an innocent eye without preconceptions. The true poet revives in himself this same capacity to see truly, to see the miracle of what really is, without being clouded by expectation or disappointment.

In this respect, the poet comes close to the saint. The saint sees the world as God sees it – and remember that we have it on scriptural authority that God saw that it was good. Truly to see the goodness of the world produces an immense happiness and I think these poems lead us to appreciate and, at their strongest, to share in the innocence of this happiness.

Snow

Louis MacNeice 1907–63

THIS IS A poem I have loved for many years. I can remember the uplift of heart I felt when reading the 'world is suddener than we fancy it' and the 'world is crazier and more of it than we think', not to mention 'the drunkenness of things being various'. The appreciation of beauty is experienced in silence and wonder; one feels in the presence of something holy.

The room was suddenly rich and the great
      bay-window was
Spawning snow and pink roses against it
Soundlessly collateral and incompatible:
World is suddener than we fancy it.

World is crazier and more of it than we think,
Incorrigibly plural. I peel and portion
A tangerine and spit the pips and feel
The drunkenness of things being various.

And the fire flames with a bubbling sound for world
Is more spiteful and gay than one supposes –
On the tongue on the eyes on the ears in the palms of
      one's hands –
There is more than glass between the snow and the
      huge roses.

Frost at Midnight

Samuel Taylor Coleridge 1772–1834

COLERIDGE FEELS his world is almost too still – 'strange and extreme silentness'. Almost in self-protection he communes with himself and then, realizing there is another present, communes with his small and sleeping son. His wistful hopes for the little boy are even more moving when we consider what the future held for Hartley Coleridge; 'all seasons' would not be sweet to him. Nevertheless I feel grateful that poor Coleridge could at least cling to the illusion that his son's life would be very different to his own. (Hartley did inherit something of his father's poetic genius, but also unfortunately something of his father's temperamental weakness.)

The Frost performs its secret ministry,
Unhelped by any wind. The owlet's cry
Came loud – and hark, again! loud as before.
The inmates of my cottage, all at rest,
Have left me to that solitude, which suits
Abstruser musings: save that at my side
My cradled infant slumbers peacefully.
'Tis calm indeed! so calm, that it disturbs
And vexes meditation with its strange
And extreme silentness. Sea, hill, and wood,
This populous village! Sea, and hill, and wood,
With all the numberless goings-on of life,
Inaudible as dreams! the thin blue flame

Lies on my low-burnt fire, and quivers not;
Only that film, which fluttered on the grate,
Still flutters there, the sole unquiet thing.
Methinks, its motion in this hush of nature
Gives it dim sympathies with me who live,
Making it a companionable form,
Whose puny flaps and freaks the idling Spirit
By its own moods interprets, every where
Echo or mirror seeking of itself,
And makes a toy of Thought.

. . .

    Dear Babe, that sleepest cradled by my side,
Whose gentle breathings, heard in this deep calm,
Fill up the intersperséd vacancies
And momentary pauses of the thought!
My babe so beautiful! it thrills my heart
With tender gladness, thus to look at thee,
And think that thou shalt learn far other lore,
And in far other scenes! For I was reared
In the great city, pent 'mid cloisters dim,
And saw nought lovely but the sky and stars.
But *thou*, my babe! shalt wander like a breeze
By lakes and sandy shores, beneath the crags
Of ancient mountain, and beneath the clouds,
Which image in their bulk both lakes and shores
And mountain crags: so shalt thou see and hear
The lovely shapes and sounds intelligible
Of that eternal language, which thy God
Utters, who from eternity doth teach

Himself in all, and all things in himself.
Great universal Teacher! he shall mould
Thy spirit, and by giving make it ask.

   Therefore all seasons shall be sweet to thee,
Whether the summer clothe the general earth
With greenness, or the redbreast sit and sing
Betwixt the tufts of snow on the bare branch
Of mossy apple-tree, while the nigh thatch
Smokes in the sun-thaw; whether the eave-drops fall
Heard only in the trances of the blast,
Or if the secret ministry of frost
Shall hang them up in silent icicles,
Quietly shining to the quiet Moon.

———— ❖❖❖ ————

Adlestrop

Edward Thomas 1878–1917

TRUTHFULNESS IS the hardest of the virtues because it demands that you have to be completely stripped of self and bare of preconceptions. Some moments you never forget, not because of anything that has happened, but because you are almost mystically aware of being alive and present – and that is what is captured in this poem. It is as if the birds are singing not by happy coincidence but to celebrate that moment.

> Yes. I remember Adlestrop –
> The name, because one afternoon
> Of heat the express-train drew up there
> Unwontedly. It was late June.
>
> The steam hissed. Someone cleared his throat.
> No one left and no one came
> On the bare platform. What I saw
> Was Adlestrop – only the name
>
> And willows, willow-herb, and grass,
> And meadowsweet, and haycocks dry,
> No whit less still and lonely fair
> Than the high cloudlets in the sky.
>
> And for that minute a blackbird sang
> Close by, and round him, mistier,
> Farther and farther, all the birds
> Of Oxfordshire and Gloucestershire.

On First Looking into Chapman's Homer
John Keats 1795–1821

THE INTELLIGENTSIA of his day sneered at Keats for not having received a classical education. Here we have the perfect example of how a lack of education can become enriching. Precisely because Keats did not know Greek and had to read Homer in Chapman's translation, he was affected to the core of his being by this most magnificent of epics. Who appreciated Homer more? The blasé scholars who could read the original, or Keats, breathless with wonder over Chapman's translation. I specially love 'wild surmise', his astonishment at the glory of Homer's *Iliad* and *Odyssey*.

Much have I travelled in the realms of gold,
    And many goodly states and kingdoms seen;
    Round many western islands have I been
Which bards in fealty to Apollo hold.
Oft of one wide expanse had I been told
    That deep-browed Homer ruled as his demesne:
    Yet did I never breathe its pure serene
Till I heard Chapman speak out loud and bold:
Then felt I like some watcher of the skies
    When a new planet swims into his ken;
Or like stout Cortez when with eagle eyes
    He stared at the Pacific – and all his men
Looked at each other with a wild surmise –
    Silent, upon a peak in Darien.

This Lunar Beauty

W. H. Auden 1907–73

AUDEN IS SPEAKING about an experience where there are no 'ghosts': all here is real, though not solid. There is a primeval sense of wonder. We have to be completely free to let great beauty move in its own way. This is wonder at its purest: the same awe we feel looking at the sea or at the stars at night. We cannot possess it and it does not belong to anything that is earthly. If one was searching for an argument for the existence of God, then it is this sense we have of unearthly wonder, wonder at something beyond anything we can encompass.

> This lunar beauty
> Has no history
> Is complete and early;
> If beauty later
> Bear any feature
> It had a lover
> And is another.
>
> This like a dream
> Keeps other time
> And daytime is
> The loss of this;
> For time is inches
> And the heart's changes
> Where ghost has haunted
> Lost and wanted.

But this was never
A ghost's endeavour
Nor finished this,
Was ghost at ease;
And till it pass
Love shall not near
The sweetness here
Nor sorrow take
His endless look.

——— ❖❖❖ ———

From

Lightenings

Seamus Heaney b. 1939

HERE IS A poem that reveals its fullness only right at
the end, when we understand that the marvellous,
out of which the man climbs, is this very ordinary world
of ours. We live in the marvellous. We just do not see it.

The annals say: when the monks of Clonmacnoise
Were all at prayers inside the oratory
A ship appeared above them in the air.

The anchor dragged along behind so deep
It hooked itself into the altar rails
And then, as the big hull rocked to a standstill,

A crewman shinned and grappled down the rope
And struggled to release it. But in vain.
'This man can't bear our life here and will drown,'

The abbot said, 'unless we help him.' So
They did, the freed ship sailed, and the man climbed
       back
Out of the marvellous as he had known it.

———— ❖❖❖ ————

The Bright Field
R. S. Thomas 1913–2000

THOMAS USES three images: the pearl of great price,
the field of great treasure and the burning bush that
Moses saw. In each case, he wants to stress that whatever
it costs in terms of what we must leave to one side, we
must pursue the treasure once we have identified it.

> I have seen the sun break through
> to illuminate a small field
> for a while, and gone my way
> and forgotten it. But that was the pearl
> of great price, the one field that had
> the treasure in it. I realise now
> that I must give all that I have
> to possess it. Life is not hurrying

on to a receding future, nor hankering after
an imagined past. It is the turning
aside like Moses to the Miracle
of the lit bush, to a brightness
that seemed as transitory as your youth
once, but is the eternity that awaits you.

———— ❖❖❖ ————

'A bird came down the walk'

Emily Dickinson 1830–86

THIS IS THE kind of poem that makes me picture
Emily Dickinson with eyes like bright beads
(though, of course, not frightened beads), like the bird she
so intently observes. The lines I love the most describe
the bird as unrolling his feathers and rowing himself soft-
ly home through the air.

A bird came down the walk:
He did not know I saw;
He bit an angle-worm in halves
And ate the fellow, raw.

And then he drank a dew
From a convenient grass,
And then hopped sidewise to the wall
To let a beetle pass.

He glanced with rapid eyes
That hurried all around –
They looked like frightened beads, I thought.
He stirred his velvet head

Like one in danger; cautious,
I offered him a crumb,
And he unrolled his feathers
And rowed him softer home

Than oars divide the ocean,
Too silver for a seam,
Or butterflies, off banks of noon,
Leap, plashless, as they swim.

———— ❖❖❖ ————

Extract from

The Prelude

William Wordsworth 1770–1850

THIS IS WORDSWORTH at his most true and responsive to the numinous in his beloved Lake District. It would be almost impertinent to call this nature poetry, but it has been called nature mysticism. Anyone who has stood alone and in silence, above all in the early morning or at night, knows the mysterious power of hills and water. Wordsworth stands alone in finding a voice for these almost indescribable feelings.

A rocky steep uprose
Above the cavern of the willow-tree,
And now, as suited one who proudly rowed
With his best skill, I fixed a steady view
Upon the top of that same craggy ridge,
The bound of the horizon – for behind
Was nothing but the stars and the grey sky.
She was an elfin pinnace; twenty times
I dipped my oars into the silent lake,
And as I rose upon the stroke my boat
Went heaving through the water like a swan –

When, from behind that rocky steep (till then
The bound of the horizon) a huge cliff,
As if with voluntary power instinct,
Upreared its head. I struck, and struck again,
And, growing still in stature, the huge cliff
Rose up between me and the stars, and still,
With measured motion, like a living thing
Strode after me. With trembling hands I turned
And through the silent water stole my way
Back to the cavern of the willow-tree.
There in her mooring-place I left my bark,
And through the meadows homeward went with grave
And serious thoughts; and after I had seen
That spectacle, for many days my brain
Worked with a dim and undetermined sense
Of unknown modes of being. In my thoughts
There was a darkness – call it solitude,

Or blank desertion. No familiar shapes
Of hourly objects, images of trees,
Of sea or sky, no colours of green fields,
But huge and mighty forms that do not live
Like living men moved slowly through my mind
By day, and were the trouble of my dreams.

———— ❖❖❖ ————

Mountains

Alice Oswald b. 1966

WORDSWORTH, who became rather crusty in old age, might not like to think that he has a daughter alive and well and speaking, with a majesty not dissimilar to his own, of the mystery of the mountains.

Something is in the line and air along edges,
which is in woods when the leaf changes
and in the leaf-pattern's gives and gauges,
the water's tension upon ledges.
Something is taken up with entrances,
which turns the issue under bridges.
The moon is between places.
An outlet fills the space between two horses.

Look through a holey stone. Now put it down.
Something is twice as different. Something gone

accumulates a queerness. Be alone.
Something is side by side with anyone.

And certain evenings, something in the balance
falls to the dewpoint where our minds condense
and then inslides itself between moments
and spills the heart from its circumference;
and this is when the moon matchlessly opens
and you can feel by instinct in the distance
the bigger mountains hidden by the mountains,
like intentions among suggestions.

————— ❖❖❖ —————

Lindenbloom

Amy Clampitt 1920–94

AMY CLAMPITT was always annoyed when she was
described as 'that woman who writes about flowers',
yet how brilliantly she captures the essence of the lime
blossom. The strollers looking up, confused by the intense
subtlety of the aroma, remain unforgettable.

> Before midsummer density
> opaques with shade the checker-
> tables underneath, in daylight
> unleafing lindens burn
> green-gold a day or two,

no more, with intimations
of an essence I saw once,
in what had been the pleasure-
garden of the popes
at Avignon, dishevel

into half (or possibly three-
quarters of) a million
hanging, intricately
tactile, blond bell-pulls
of bloom, the in-mid-air
resort of honeybees'
hirsute cotillion
teasing by the milligram
out of those necklaced
nectaries, aromas

so intensely subtle,
strollers passing under
looked up confused,
as though they'd just
heard voices, or
inhaled the ghost
of derelict splendor
and/or of seraphs shaken
into pollen dust

no transubstantiating
pope or antipope could sift
or quite precisely ponder.

Clouds

Denise Levertov 1923–97

DENISE LEVERTOV was a superb letter-writer and the very extensive correspondence between her and her fellow poet Robert Duncan often show us the circumstances, or even just the emotions, from which her poetry sprang. Here the alternation between 'I' and 'We' and the continual references to cold and death foreshadow the dying relationship with her husband. 'But I forced to mind my vision of a sky': it was her wonder at the extraordinary beauty and subtlety of nature that sustained her.

> The clouds as I see them, rising
> urgently, roseate in the
> mounting of somber power
>
> surging in evening haste over
> roofs and hermetic
> grim walls –
>
>   Last night
> As if death had lit a pale light
> in your flesh, your flesh
> was cold to my touch, or not cold
> but cool, cooling, as if the last traces
> of warmth were still fading in you.

My thigh burned in cold fear where
yours touched it.

But I forced to mind my vision of a sky
close and enclosed, unlike the space in which
        these clouds move –
a sky of gray mist it appeared –
and how looking intently at it we saw
its gray was not gray but a milky white
in which radiant traces of opal greens,
fiery blues, gleamed, faded, gleamed again,
and how only then, seeing the color in the gray,
a field sprang into sight, extending
between where we stood and the horizon,
a field of freshest deep spiring grass
starred with dandelions,
green and gold
gold and green alternating in closewoven
chords, madrigal field.

Is death's chill that visited our bed
other than what it seemed, is it
a gray to be watched keenly?

Wiping my glasses and leaning westward,
clearing my mind of the day's mist and leaning
into myself to see
the colors of truth

I watch the clouds as I see them

in pomp advancing, pursuing
the fallen sun.

——— ❖❖❖ ———

'Loveliest of trees, the cherry now'
A. E. Housman 1859–1936

'LOVELIEST OF TREES' is also, surely, amongst the loveliest of verses. It comes from Housman's best-known poem, *A Shropshire Lad*. Where will we find a more lyrical expression of the need to have time and space, truly to appreciate the wonder of the natural world?

Loveliest of trees, the cherry now
Is hung with bloom along the bough,
And stands about the woodland ride
Wearing white for Eastertide.

Now, of my threescore years and ten,
Twenty will not come again,
And take from seventy springs a score,
It only leaves me fifty more.

And since to look at things in bloom
Fifty springs are little room,
About the woodlands I will go
To see the cherry hung with snow.

A LIGHTER SPIRIT

— ❖ ❖ ❖ —

ALTHOUGH MANY of these poems make me laugh aloud and all make me smile, they are not what I would call 'comic verse'. Comic verse certainly has its place. Robust and good-natured, it is the poetic equivalent of the delights of Agatha Christie's thrillers. The poems I have chosen have a far more serious intent: they share truth with us in a light-hearted and, in the old sense of the word, gay, manner.

It is extraordinarily difficult to write a poem that is light of heart: one that genuinely pleases and amuses and yet is not trivial. The curse of triviality awaits all who approach the muse with a daffodil (or even a daisy) and an insouciant wave of the hand. The muse prefers to be wooed in a more serious manner, knee-bowed and eyes aflame with devotion. So I cherish the poets who achieve the feat of laughing and singing at the same time.

It seems to me that none of these light-hearted poems need any comment for our enjoyment and under-standing, except 'Welsh Incident' by Robert Graves, and then only to say that it really needs to be read in a Welsh voice. I am advised it is rather too long for the anthology, but it makes me laugh out loud every time I read it.

Welsh Incident

Robert Graves 1895–1985

'But that was nothing to what things came out
From the sea-caves of Criccieth yonder.'
'What were they? Mermaids? dragons? ghosts?'
'Nothing at all of any things like that.'
'What were they, then?'
               'All sorts of queer things,
Things never seen or heard or written about,
Very strange, un-Welsh, utterly peculiar
Things. Oh, solid enough they seemed to touch,
Had anyone dared it. Marvellous creation,
All various shapes and sizes, and no sizes,
All new, each perfectly unlike his neighbour,
Though all came moving slowly out together.'
'Describe just one of them.'
               'I am unable.'
'What were their colours?'
               'Mostly nameless colours,
Colours you'd like to see; but one was puce
Or perhaps more like crimson, but not purplish.
Some had no colour.'
               'Tell me, had they legs?'
'Not a leg nor foot among them that I saw.'
'But did these things come out in any order?
What o'clock was it? What was the day of the week?
Who else was present? How was the weather?'
'I was coming to that. It was half-past three

46

On Easter Tuesday last. The sun was shining.
The Harlech Silver Band played *Marchog Jesu*
On thirty-seven shimmering instruments
Collecting for Caernarvon's (Fever) Hospital Fund.
The populations of Pwllheli, Criccieth,
Portmadoc, Borth, Tremadoc, Penrhyndeudraeth,
Were all assembled. Criccieth's mayor addressed them
First in good Welsh and then in fluent English,
Twisting his fingers in his chain of office,
Welcoming the things. They came out on the sand,
Not keeping time to the band, moving seaward
Silently at a snail's pace. But at last
The most odd, indescribable thing of all,
Which hardly one man there could see for wonder,
Did something recognizably a something.'
'Well, what?'
                'It made a noise.'
                                'A frightening noise?'
'No, no.'
        'A musical noise? A noise of scuffling?'
'No, but a very loud, respectable noise –
Like groaning to oneself on Sunday morning
In Chapel, close before the second psalm.'
'What did the mayor do?'
                        'I was coming to that'.

Confession, 1931

Carl Rakosi 1903–2004

And now the young followers
of Pound close ranks,
I among them,
and wish to be heard.

As a populist
I wish to proceed
with serious dignity
thus: 'My fellow townsmen, etc.'

but I have a hornpipe
in my head
kicking up its heels
and wanting out

but delicately,
as if a butterfly had flown
out of the English language.

Silence

Marianne Moore 1887–1972

My father used to say,
'Superior people never make long visits,
have to be shown Longfellow's grave
or the glass flowers at Harvard.
Self-reliant like the cat –
that takes its prey to privacy,
the mouse's limp tail hanging like a shoelace
     from its mouth –

they sometimes enjoy solitude,
and can be robbed of speech
by speech which has delighted them.
The deepest feeling always shows itself in silence;
and in silence, but restraint.'
Nor was he insincere in saying, 'Make my
     house your inn.'
Inns are not residences.

Can You Imagine?

Mary Oliver b. 1935

For example, what the trees do
not only in lightening storms
or the watery dark of a summer's night
or under the white nets of winter
but now, and now, and now – whenever
we're not looking. Surely you can't imagine
they don't dance, from the root up, wishing
to travel a little, not cramped so much as wanting
a better view, or more sun, or just as avidly
more shade – surely you can't imagine they just
stand there loving every
minute of it, the birds or the emptiness, the dark
      rings
of the years slowly and without a sound
thickening, and nothing different unless the wind,
and then only in its own mood, comes
to visit, surely you can't imagine
patience, and happiness, like that.

Humming-Bird

D. H. Lawrence 1885–1930

I can imagine, in some otherworld
Primeval-dumb, far back
In that most awful stillness, that only gasped and
    hummed,
Humming-birds raced down the avenues.

Before anything had a soul,
While life was a heave of Matter, half inanimate,
This little bit chipped off in brilliance
And went whizzing through the slow, vast, succulent
    stems.

I believe there were no flowers then,
In the world where the humming-bird flashed ahead
    of creation.
I believe he pierced the slow vegetable veins with his
    long beak.

Probably he was big
As mosses, and little lizards, they say, were once big.
Probably he was a jabbing, terrifying monster.

We look at him through the wrong end of the long
    telescope of Time,
Luckily for us.

Advice

Robert Crawford b. 1959

When you are faced with two alternatives
Choose both. And should they put you to the test,
Tick every box. Nothing is ever single.
A seed's a tree's a ship's a constellation.
Nail your true colours to this branching mast

———— ❖❖❖ ————

Fiddle-Faddle

John Hollander b. 1929

there are things that are important beyond all this fiddle
Marianne Moore, 'Poetry'

Well, all *that* fiddle
perhaps. But not this
sublime faddle, far
    more important

than whatever 'this
fiddle' might have been
(although granted not
    the resonant

machine of spruce and
maple that we need
   to hear certain
kinds of truth with).

Fiddle can sound as
   if it had a
silly middle and
were thereby of use

flying and sighing
intonations have
shaped all that faddle
in its final form.

Well, then the death of
all that importance
   incident to
the fiddler's own death

– the body, the mind
with their pains and woes
their cares and delights
   their assessments

of what matters most
all fled – the faddle
   will settle down
in its newly found

place in existence,
played and playing, sung
and singing, ever
     shaping anew

the sounds of what is
seen, the lights and shades
of what is heard, and
     thereby giving

some previously
inconceivable
     new meaning to
importance itself.

———— ❖❖❖ ————

Tenuous and Precarious

Stevie Smith 1902–71

Tenuous and Precarious
Were my guardians,
Precarious and Tenuous,
Two Romans.

My father was Hazardous,
Hazardous,
Dear old man,
Three Romans.

There was my brother Spurious,
Spurious Posthumous,
Spurious was spurious
Was four Romans.

My husband was Perfidious,
He was perfidious.
Five Romans.

Surreptitious, our son,
Was surreptitious,
He was six Romans.

Our cat Tedious
Still lives,
Count not Tedious
Yet.

My name is Finis,
Finis, Finis,
I am Finis,
Six, five, four, three, two,
One Roman,
Finis.

THE HEAVY
HEART

———❖❖❖———

I T WOULD BE escapist, I fear, to enjoy the poetry of the smile unless we were equally willing to enjoy poetry that frowns or even weeps. Temperamentally I am not given to what we could term 'the dark stuff', but I did find when collecting poems solely on the basis of what I responded to that there were quite a few poets whose work I classified under 'anger'. Anger turned out to be too small a concept. Hate revealed itself as equally powerful a motivating force. What was not created in the fierce furnace of wrath seemed to come to us from the deep freeze of hatred. Horrible emotions both, yet to what powerful poetry they have given rise. If we read these poems without a sad sense of fellowship, we are not reading truthfully.

One of the painful effects of great art is to force us to confront the darkness within ourselves, that heaviness of spirit that will drag us downwards if we allow it. We all have the capacity for anger, hate, envy and all the hideous limitations of the self-centred spirit. Perhaps here in these great poems we can find not just humiliation but catharsis. The great Greek tragedians offered their audience precisely this catharsis: the purifying of the spirit by grief and fear. Although I certainly make no such claim for these short poems, I think it is that to which they aspire.

A Poison Tree

William Blake 1757–1827

BLAKE WAS NOT the sweet innocent one might think. He was capable of hatred and this poem about anger against an enemy proffers a warning that you can destroy an enemy but in doing so you will destroy yourself. Bitterness is the most destructive of emotions. I tremble at this poem, at the sheer nastiness of using your enemy's own evil (his desire for your apple) against him.

> I was angry with my friend:
> I told my wrath, my wrath did end.
> I was angry with my foe:
> I told it not, my wrath did grow.
>
> And I water'd it in fears,
> Night and morning with my tears;
> And I sunned it with smiles,
> And with soft deceitful wiles.
>
> And it grew both day and night,
> Till it bore an apple bright;
> And my foe beheld it shine,
> And he knew that it was mine,
>
> And into my garden stole
> When the night had veil'd the pole:
> In the morning glad I see
> My foe outstretch'd beneath the tree.

The Wrong Beds (after Baudelaire)
Roger McGough b. 1937

RAILING AGAINST the difficulties of our lives is futile.
The best the poet can manage is angry acceptance.

Life is a hospital ward, and the beds we are put in
are the ones we don't want to be in.
We'd get better sooner if put over by the window
Or by the radiator, one could suffer easier there.

At night, the impatient soul dreams of faraway places.
The Aegean: all marble and light. Where, upon a beach
as flat as a map, you could bask in the sun like
    a lizard.

The Pole: where, bathing in darkness, you could watch
the sparks from Hell reflected in a sky of ice.
The soul could be happier anywhere than where it
    happens to be.

Anywhere but here. We take our medicine daily,
nod politely, and grumble occasionally.
But it is out of our hands. Always the wrong place.
We didn't make our beds, but we lie in them.

Castalian Spring

Seamus Heaney b. 1939

HEANEY EXPRESSES powerfully the anger of a thwarted will. He feels himself justified by the nobility of his desire to drink of the waters of poetry. This suggests he is writing about a creative block. He is determined to drink from the spring, yet he cannot get to the waters because they are roped off from him. He feels his poetic impotence is not his fault, but the fault of whoever denies him the sacred waters of inspiration.

Thunderface. Not Zeus's ire, but hers
Refusing entry, and mine mounting from it.
This one thing I had vowed: to drink the waters
Of the Castalian Spring, to arrogate
That much to myself and be the poet
Under the God Apollo's giddy cliff –
But the inner water sanctum was roped off
When we arrived. Well then, to hell with that,
And to hell with all who'd stop me, thunderface!
So up the steps then, into the sandstone grottoes,
The seeps and dreeps, the shallow pools, the mosses,
Come from beyond, and come far, with this useless
Anger draining away, on terraces
Where I bowed and mouthed in sweetness and
        defiance.

Fire and Ice

Robert Frost 1874–1963

YOU CAN destroy yourself by fire – by anger expressed outwards – as well as by coldness turned inwards. You will notice that this is not a choice. You either hate too much or love too much.

> Some say the world will end in fire,
> Some say in ice.
> From what I've tasted of desire
> I hold with those who favour fire.
>
> But if it had to perish twice,
> I think I know enough of hate
> To say that for destruction ice
> Is also great
> And would suffice.

Waiting for the Barbarians
C. P. Cavafy 1863–1933

Translated by Edmund Keeley and Philip Sherrard

THIS IS A famous poem, about sullen despair at being without direction. When the external answer is removed, the weak (whom Cavafy identifies as all of us) are left floundering.

What are we waiting for, assembled in the forum?

The barbarians are due here today.

Why isn't anything going on the senate?
Why are the senators sitting there without legislating?

Because the barbarians are coming today.
What's the point of senators making laws now?
Once the barbarians are here, they'll do the legislating.

Why did our emperor get up so early,
and why is he sitting enthroned at the city's main gate,
in state, wearing the crown?

Because the barbarians are coming today
and the emperor's waiting to receive their leader.
He's even got a scroll to give him,
loaded with titles, with imposing names.

Why have our two consuls and praetors come out today
wearing their embroidered, their scarlet togas?
Why have they put on bracelets with so many
    amethysts,
rings sparkling with magnificent emeralds?
Why are they carrying elegant canes
beautifully worked in silver and gold?

    Because the barbarians are coming today
    and things like that dazzle the barbarians.

Why don't our distinguished orators turn up as usual
to make their speeches, say what they have to say?

    Because the barbarians are coming today
    and they're bored by rhetoric and public speaking.

Why this sudden bewilderment, this confusion?
(How serious people's faces have become.)
Why are the streets and squares emptying so rapidly,
everyone going home lost in thought?

    Because night has fallen and the barbarians haven't
      come.
    And some of our men just in from the border say
    there are no barbarians any longer.

Now what's going to happen to us without
    barbarians?
Those people were a kind of solution.

Walking Past a Rose this June Morning
Alice Oswald b. 1966

I HAVE A GREAT affection for the poetry of Alice Oswald, and she expresses with brilliant immediacy the sense of being trapped. I feel we ache with her, held without escape in suffocating constriction.

is my heart a rose? how unspeakable
is my heart a rose? how unspeakable
is my heart folded to dismantle? how unspeakable
is a rose folded in its nerves? how unspeakable
is my heart secretly overhanging us? pause
is there a new world known only to breathing?
now inhale what I remember. pause. how unbreathable

this is my heart out. how unspeakable
this is my risen skin. how unthinkable
this is my tense touch-sensitive heart
this is its mass made springy by the rain
this loosening compression of hope. how unworkable
is an invisible ray lighting up your lungs? how invisible?
is it a weightless rapture? pause. how weightless?

now trace a breath-map in the air. how invisible?
is a rose a turning cylinder of senses? how unspeakable
is this the ghost of the heart, the actual
the inmost deceleration of its thought? how unspeakable
is everything still speeding around us? pause
is my heart the centre? how unbearable
is the rain a halo? how unbearable

Carentan O Carentan

Louis Simpson b. 1923

THIS POEM always seems to me a contemporary ballad, a narrative that slowly reveals itself to be about death and the destruction of war as the bewildered young soldier discovers that he is the only living creature in a landscape of death.

Trees in the old days used to stand
And shape a shady lane
Where lovers wandered hand in hand
Who came from Carentan.

This was the shining green canal
Where we came two by two
Walking at combat-interval.
Such trees we never knew.

The day was early June, the ground
Was soft and bright with dew.
Far away the guns did sound,
But here the sky was blue.

The sky was blue, but there a smoke
Hung still above the sea
Where the ships together spoke
To towns we could not see.

Could you have seen us through a glass
You would have said a walk
Of farmers out to turn the grass,
Each with his own hay-fork.

The watchers in their leopard suits
Waited till it was time,
And aimed between the belt and boot
And let the barrel climb.

I must lie down at once, there is
A hammer at my knee.
And call it death or cowardice,
Don't count again on me.

Everything's all right, Mother,
Everyone gets the same
At one time or another.
It's all in the game.

I never strolled, nor ever shall,
Down such a leafy lane.
I never drank in a canal,
Nor ever shall again.

There is a whistling in the leaves
And it is not the wind,
The twigs are falling from the knives
That cut men to the ground.

Tell me, Master-Sergeant,
The way to turn and shoot.
But the Sergeant's silent
That taught me how to do it.

O Captain, show us quickly
Our place upon the map.
But the Captain's sickly
And taking a long nap.

Lieutenant, what's my duty,
My place in the platoon?
He too's a sleeping beauty,
Charmed by that strange tune.

Carentan O Carentan
Before we met with you
We never yet had lost a man
Or known what death could do.

———— ❖❖❖ ————

A Censor Complains

Alasdair Gray b. 1934

THIS IS a despairing poem about how a civilization can destroy itself. Once you start dreading the truth and destroying the poets you cannot retrieve the history

that has been lost. This is what it means to have a censor:
to be protected from the truths we do not want to hear.

Each day lays down more past to be digested, blended
in memory through the ministry
of sleep and dream.

Each poem leaves more truth to be digested, blended
in history through the ministry
of speech and print.

Born by a revolution, my regime
sprang from words, made history, held it tight,
dreaded more truth

so poets dumbed or died or fled abroad.
Only they knew the truths I silenced
better than me.

My regime died of dull language.
I cannot now give out what I withheld.
A new regime thinks truth cheap, the past
        unimportant.
The young agree.

Fanfaronade

Carole Coates b. 1943

O NE CAN READ this poem several ways. Is it about a woman caught in a relationship with a man, which she sees – too late – is oppressive? Or is she caught in a political situation from which she cannot escape? With the glorious economy of the true poet, Coates makes both meanings relevant simultaneously and we move with her through incredulous amusement at the sheer ego of the 'him' to a panicky sense of being caught in a relentless grip. She sees through the eyes of others, yet it has not saved her.

If I had left sooner

(I could have done –
I had decided to run.)

Then I saw him proceeding
in the slow procession
of himself, coming nearer.

He should have ridden an elephant:
it was consequence, magnitude
and everyone believed it.

He should have been first in a parade of elephants:
jumbos with howdahs and popinjays and tassels –
amplitude, orotundity – that sort of procession.

There must have been fanfares of trumpets:
even though I couldn't hear them
my ear drums rattled and spun.

The fanfaronade came nearer:
the profile, the gestures, the nabob pose –
many believed it and stayed.

I should have left sooner:
But the roads were all closed
Because of the vast parade.

COURAGE

—❖❖❖—

I AM NOT THINKING here primarily of the bold, risk-taking courage that wins the Victoria Cross and may flair magnificently once only. What I have in mind is quiet courage: the bravery of endurance which most of us have met fairly frequently and have been so encouraged (forgive the pun) by such daily examples of heroism. This is the courage of the cancer victim, of those damaged by war or accident, those suffering under the painful sense of their own inability to achieve the goals on which they have set their hearts. There is nothing flashy here, nothing perhaps to catch the eye. But I cannot sufficiently admire the nobility of those who will not whine or repine, will not make excuses, will not escape into a mental dishonesty, keeping their heart high and holding to the truth amidst all the suffering life can throw at them: this seems to be courage of the highest sort. I salute it and long to emulate it.

Fidele

William Shakespeare 1564–1616

SHAKESPEARE IS often deceptively simple, and the idea expressed here with such lyricism is a profound one: to approach death means to be removed from fear. We must all die, and on death we will all receive the enormous blessing that every threat and sorrow is at an end.

Fear no more the heat o' the sun,
Nor the furious winter's rages;
Thou thy worldly task hast done,
Home art gone, and ta'en thy wages:
Golden lads and girls all must,
As chimney-sweepers, come to dust.

Fear no more the frown o' the great,
Thou art past the tyrant's stroke;
Care no more to clothe and eat;
To thee the reed is as the oak:
The sceptre, learning, physic, must
All follow this, and come to dust.

Fear no more the lightning-flash,
Nor the all-dreaded thunder-stone;
Fear not slander, censure rash;
Thou hast finish'd joy and moan:
All lovers young, all lovers must
Consign to thee, and come to dust.

No exorciser harm thee!
　　Nor no witchcraft charm thee!
Ghost unlaid forbear thee!
　　Nothing ill come near thee!
Quiet consummation have;
And renownèd be thy grave!

———— ❖❖❖ ————

'Because I could not stop for death'

Emily Dickinson 1830–86

IN AN IMAGE of wonderful simplicity and peace, Dickinson admits the inevitability of death and accepts that her destination, like our own, is the grave. I thrill especially to the word of hope with which she ends: the grave is not the entrance to nothingness but to eternity.

Because I could not stop for Death,
He kindly stopped for me;
The carriage held but just ourselves
And Immortality.

We slowly drove, he knew no haste,
And I had put away
My labor, and my leisure too,
For his civility.

We passed the school, where children strove
At recess, in the ring;
We passed the fields of gazing grain,
We passed the setting sun.

Or rather, he passed us;
The dews grew quivering and chill,
For only gossamer my gown,
My tippet only tulle.

We paused before a house that seemed
A swelling of the ground;
The roof was scarcely visible,
The cornice in the ground.

Since then 'tis centuries, and yet
Feels shorter than the day
I first surmised the horses' heads
Were toward eternity.

The Lights are on Everywhere
Charles Simic b. 1938

IN THIS TOPSY-TURVY world of chaos and falsity, people still endure, even though everything here speaks of despair. Everywhere there are lies and deception, as though confiscating clocks and watches will change the time or painting sunrises will make it morning. There is darkness and violence on all sides and no amount of scrubbing can wipe the stains away. Yet the very ability to formulate this, not to accept the lies or violence, is what this poem is about. It articulates a great disgust for war and politics and it is this refusal that is so heartening.

> The Emperor must not be told night is coming.
> His armies are chasing shadows,
> Arresting whippoorwills and hermit thrushes
> And setting towns and villages on fire.
>
> In the capital, they go around confiscating
> Clocks and watches, burning heretics,
> And painting the sunrise over the rooftops
> While the people wish each other good morning.
>
> The rooster brought in chains is crowing,
> The flowers in the garden have been made to stay open,
> And still dark stains appear on palace floors
> Which no amount of scrubbing can wipe away.

A Clear Day and No Memories
Wallace Stevens 1879–1955

WALLACE STEVENS was in his seventies when he wrote this poem and there is a sense of a man 'clearing the decks'. As he comes to the end of a life that has been rich in experience, he refuses to look back or repine. There is almost exhilaration in the dignity and peace with which he accepts the inevitable end.

No soldiers in the scenery,
No thoughts of people now dead,
As they were fifty years ago:
Young and living in a live air,
Young and walking in the sunshine,
Bending in blue dresses to touch something –
Today the mind is not part of the weather.

Today the air is clear of everything.
It has no knowledge except of nothingness
And it flows over us without meanings,
As if none of us had ever been here before
And are not now: in this shallow spectacle,
This invisible activity, this sense.

Door

Robert Pinsky b. 1940

A LL PINSKY CAN do is let in his little companion. The
doors of perception are so numerous, too many to
cleanse. He has given up trying to see through them, but
we know he will survive.

> The cat cries for me from the other side.
> It is beyond her to work this device
> That I open and cross and close
> With such ease when I mean to work.
>
> Its four panels form a cross – the rood,
> Sign of suffering and redemption.
> The rod, a dividing pike or pale
> Mounted and hinged to swing between
>
> One way or place and another, meow.
> Between the January vulva of birth
> And the January of death's door
> There are so many to negotiate,
>
> Closed or flung open or ajar, valves
> Of attention. O kitty, if the doors
> Of perception were cleansed
> All things would appear as they are,

Infinite. Come in, darling, drowse
Comfortably near my feet, I will click
The barrier closed again behind you, O
Sister will, fellow-mortal, here we are.

———— ❖❖❖ ————

Disturbing the Tarantula
Christopher Middleton b. 1926

THIS POEM COULD very well have gone under 'The
Heavy Heart' because it tackles the problem of our
secret fears, but I think it tackles them with such
courage, such acceptance of the dark things lurking
within us and such a refusal to ignore them or pretend
that the world is different from what it is, that I cannot
but hail the poet's bravery.

> The door a maze
> of shadow, peach leaves
> veining its wood colour,
>
> and cobwebs broken
> breathing ah ah
> as it is pushed open –
>
> two hands
> at a ladder shook
> free the tarantula, it slid

black and fizzing to a rung
above eye-level,
knees jack knives,

a high-jumper's, bat mouth
slit grinning
into the fur belly –

helpful: peaches
out there, they keep growing
rounder and rounder

on branches wheeled low
by their weight over
roasted grass blades; sun

and moon, also, evolve
round this mountain
terrace, wrinkling now

with deadly green
emotion: All things
are here, monstrous convulsed

rose (don't anyone
dare come), sounding through
our caves, I hear them.

Archaic Torso of Apollo

Rainer Maria Rilke 1875–1926

Translated by Martin Greenberg

YOU DO NOT look at great art for simple entertainment or, in an ordinary sense, pleasure. The real blessing is that it draws you into something greater than yourself, not something alien, but something within yourself.

We never knew his extraordinary head,
with swelling stone eyeballs. Yet even broken,
his torso still glows like a lighted lantern
in which his gaze, damped down, not out, not dead,

keeps burning on. Or else the breast's bent bow
could never dazzle you, nor yet a smile run
ruffling through the loins' slight subtle flexion
to that midpoint from which ourselves we sow.

Or else the stone would be a stump, cut off
beneath the shoulders' clear transparent drop,
and wouldn't glisten like a wild beast's coat;

and wouldn't, breaking through the outlines of itself,
glitter like a star: for in it no least part
but finds you out. You've got to change your life.

Sailing to Byzantium
W. B. Yeats 1865–1939

THIS IS ONE of the great poems about what it means to be old and to long to be changed into something that will endure, to be not mortal flesh but a mystical permanence. Yeats sings about sailing to the Eastern sages, where he will be transformed, where they will come to him from 'the holy fire' and enclose him in a mystical circle ('perne in a gyre'). He longs for a singing master to teach him how to transcend what he is and become something eternal and non-human.

I

That is no country for old men. The young
In one another's arms, birds in the trees
– Those dying generations – at their song,
The salmon-falls, the mackerel-crowded seas,
Fish, flesh, or fowl, commend all summer long
Whatever is begotten, born, and dies.
Caught in that sensual music all neglect
Monuments of unageing intellect.

II

An aged man is but a paltry thing,
A tattered coat upon a stick, unless
Soul clap its hands and sing, and louder sing
For every tatter in its mortal dress,
Nor is there singing school but studying

Monuments of its own magnificence;
And therefore I have sailed the seas and come
To the holy city of Byzantium.

III

O sages standing in God's holy fire
As in the gold mosaic of a wall,
Come from the holy fire, perne in a gyre,
And be the singing-masters of my soul.
Consume my heart away; sick with desire
And fastened to a dying animal
It knows not what it is; and gather me
Into the artifice of eternity.

IV

Once out of nature I shall never take
My bodily form from any natural thing,
But such a form as Grecian goldsmiths make
Of hammered gold and gold enamelling
To keep a drowsy Emperor awake;
Or set upon a golden bough to sing
To lords and ladies of Byzantium
Of what is past, or passing, or to come.

Feofan Grek: The Novgorod Frescoes
Rowan Williams b. 1950

As the Archbishop of Canterbury, by definition a man of God, Rowan Williams knows what it means to be a sage standing in the divine fire. He wonders, though, whether Yeats understood the implications of what he asks for in 'Sailing to Byzantium'. I pick up a gentle suggestion that when we use an image we must do so with a real acceptance of its implications. The frescoes referred to in the poem are in the Cathedral of the Transfiguration in Novgorod, 100 miles to the south of St Petersburg.

Did Yeats mean this? because when sages
stand in the fire, this happens. Skin
umbers and cracks and shines. And then
on hands, shoulders and skirts, the splash
and dribble; you could think the bells have melted
    from their perch,
so that the roaring hollows fall, lazy as snow,
bright liquid pebbles. And then, long
after the eyes have gone, the cheekbones
gleam, razored with little scars in parallel,
the surgery of initiation, letting through
furnaces under the dun hard skin.
We slow down more and more as the heat rises;
    surfaces
dry up, something inside swells painfully.
The razor makes its first cut. From the oven walls,
out of the searing dusk, they smile
(not at us) blindly.

Among the Narcissi
Sylvia Plath 1932–63

ALTHOUGH I OFTEN find Sylvia Plath over-dramatic and self-regarding, this poem moves me with its objectivity and sympathy. She is looking at an old man, whom she knows to be recovering from an operation, and notices how the flowers seem in sympathy with him: as the wind bends them over, lays them flat on the earth, so life has bent him over. There is even a subliminal suggestion that, like the narcissi, he will not be wholly extinguished.

Spry, wry, and gray as these March sticks,
Percy bows, in his blue peajacket, among the narcissi.
He is recuperating from something on the lung.

The narcissi, too, are bowing to some big thing:
It rattles their stars on the green hill where Percy
Nurses the hardship of his stitches, and walks and
    walks.

There is a dignity to this; there is a formality –
The flowers vivid as bandages, and the man mending.
They bow and stand: they suffer such attacks!

And the octogenarian loves the little flocks.
He is quite blue; the terrible wind tries his breathing.
The narcissi look up like children, quickly and
    whitely.

Old Mr Forrester

Josephine Jacobsen 1908–2003

THIS IS A wonderful description of old age and of the failure of the body to respond to the will. What interests Jacobsen most is that poor old Mr Forrester has not cultivated his inner life. The sheer pressures of our contemporary world have protected him at every stage from reality and she imagines this aged gentleman trying to come to terms with the realization that he has a soul.

Old Mr Forrester – light, light as a leaf,
Brown, desiccated, and attached by just
The thinnest stem to motion and the sun.
He sat all day in the precious, vanishing warmth
And watched his feet in black and shining shoes,
And watched his dry, blotched, unaspiring hands,
And now and then the far heights of the mountains.
And meditated, perhaps, upon his body:
That most familiar and disobedient thing,
Which in time segments was his abject slave,
Dressed as he willed, raised, lowered, hot or cold,
But in the sweep, the arc disclosing itself,
Altering with silent mutiny each particle
The will asserted was his own: the hair,
Changing without request its original color,
The muscles, unauthorized, loosening their grip,
The teeth deserting, the eyes treacherous, and
The lazy blood

Slack in its flowing and unpunishable.
And meditated, perhaps, upon his soul –
Which meant heaven knew what – the inner thing
With which he had incuriously lived
Until the prospect of its company
On a trip into territory where this would be
Presumably the Friend to Have, the *Visé*,
The Contact, made him desire to cultivate
An alien whose speech he did not know
And the long residence of whose proximity
Might make him now a sullen and suspicious
Prospect for this belated amity.

———— ❖❖❖ ————

The Bridge

Ruth Pitter 1897–1992

S ORROW CAN BE overwhelming but Pitter is convinced
that it is not the deepest reality. This is an immensely
courageous poem about the need to go forward into the
unknown, to recognize that there always is a bridge and
that we can cross it to find that truth that is more real
than sorrow.

Where is the truth that will inform my sorrow?
I am sure myself that sorrow is not the truth.
These lovely shapes of sorrow are empty vessels
Waiting for wine: they wait to be informed.
Men make the vessels on either side of the river;
On this the hither side the artists make them,
And there over the water the workmen make them:
These frail, with a peacock glaze, and the others
      heavy,
Simple as doom, made to endure the furnace.
War shatters the peacock-jars: let us go over.

Indeed we have no choice but to go over.

There is always a way for those who must go over:
Always a bridge from the known to the unknown.
When from the known the mind revolts and despairs
There lies the way, and there we must go over.

O truth, is it death there over the river,
Or is it life, new life in a land of summer?
The mind is an empty vessel, a shape of sorrow,
Fill it with life or death, for it is hollow,
Dark wine or bright, fill it, let us go over.

Let me go find my truth, over the river.

Epilogue

Robert Lowell 1917–77

HERE LOWELL IS grappling painfully with his in-
ability to create, to rise from remembrance to
imagination. He longs to have in his poetry the light that
Vermeer revealed so subtly and so beautifully in his
painting. Vermeer painted a world that Lowell mourns
and can do little more than photograph.

Those blessèd structures, plot and rhyme –
why are they no help to me now
I want to make
something imagined, not recalled?
I hear the noise of my own voice:
The painter's vision is not a lens,
it trembles to caress the light.
But sometimes everything I write
with the threadbare art of my eye
seems a snapshot,
lurid, rapid, garish, grouped,
heightened from life,
yet paralyzed by fact.
All's misalliance.
Yet why not say what happened?
Pray for the grace of accuracy
Vermeer gave to the sun's illumination
stealing like the tide across a map
to his girl solid with yearning.

We are poor passing facts,
warned by that to give
each figure in the photograph
his living name.

SORROW

NO ONE HAS EVER lived who has not known sorrow. It does not come unadulterated, of course. There are always chinks of light in the darkness. Nor is it always necessarily a bad thing. We can learn from our sorrow. In fact, we must learn from it, because it will be part of our lives and surely the greatest sorrow of all would be to have wasted the opportunities that sadness brings us. When a parent is grieving over the death of a child or a husband over a beloved wife, it can seem almost heartless to remind them that death and loss are part of being human and that (forgive me) we almost invalidate this precious death if we let it tear us apart instead of accepting it as an inevitable consequence of our mortality.

Moreover, since no one has ever lived and been blameless, all of us must have occasion to repent. I am not talking about guilt, which can hang albatross-like around a neck and weigh one down fruitlessly, nor am I talking about remorse, that debilitating emotion that eats us up with a sense of the horrible 'done-ness' of a past act. It is done. It cannot be redone. It stays there like a stone. Our mind goes round and round lamenting. This achieves nothing and if there are poems commemorating this useless misery I neither know them nor wish to know them.

Repentance is a very different experience. It acknowledges the inevitability of the past, accepting it and moving forward. It is one of the manifestations of sorrow with which I hope we have all made friends.

One Art

Elizabeth Bishop 1911–79

BISHOP BRILLIANTLY accustoms us to loss by starting us off with small things and letting them get bigger and bigger and bigger. In 'One Art' the loss is literal, as we might suspect. She did indeed lose two cities (New York and Rio) when her Brazilian lover died, nor was there a place for her any longer in 'a continent' (South America). It is a deeply stoical poem, admitting that we are going to lose all that makes life precious to us and still survive. It is also a very powerful way of speaking about emotional disaster, while not succumbing to it.

The art of losing isn't hard to master;
so many things seem filled with the intent
to be lost that their loss is no disaster.

Lose something every day. Accept the fluster
of lost door keys, the hour badly spent.
The art of losing isn't hard to master.

Then practice losing farther, losing faster:
places, and names, and where it was you meant
to travel. None of these will bring disaster.

I lost my mother's watch. And look! my last, or
next-to-last, of three loved houses went.
The art of losing isn't hard to master.

I lost two cities, lovely ones. And, vaster,
some realms I owned, two rivers, a continent.
I miss them, but it wasn't a disaster.

– Even losing you (the joking voice, a gesture
I love) I shan't have lied. It's evident
the art of losing's not too hard to master
though it may look like (*Write* it!) like disaster.

❖❖❖

Musée des Beaux Arts
W. H. Auden 1907–73

THIS POEM IS not about an experience of suffering, rather Auden takes an objective look at how one man's tragedy is another's inconvenience and how brilliantly this terrifying insight is made visible to us by great painters. When we suffer, we feel it subdues the whole world to its intensity and importance. It is not so, and this is hard to accept.

About suffering they were never wrong,
The Old Masters: how well they understood
Its human position; how it takes place
While someone else is eating or opening a window or
    just walking dully along;

How, when the aged are reverently, passionately
      waiting
For the miraculous birth, there always must be
Children who did not specially want it to happen,
      skating
On a pond at the edge of the wood:
They never forgot
That even the dreadful martyrdom must run its course
Anyhow in a corner, some untidy spot
Where the dogs go on with their doggy life and the
      torturer's horse
Scratches its innocent behind on a tree.

In Brueghel's *Icarus*, for instance: how everything turns
      away
Quite leisurely from the disaster; the ploughman may
Have heard the splash, the forsaken cry,
But for him it was not an important failure; the sun
      shone
As it had to on the white legs disappearing into the
      green
Water; and the expensive delicate ship that must have
      seen
Something amazing, a boy falling out of the sky,
 Had somewhere to get to and sailed calmly on.

'Success is counted sweetest'
Emily Dickinson 1830–86

I FIND A DEEP empathy with the dying man, hearing the jubilation of the victors. This is an instance where Emily Dickinson goes right to the heart of something, very poignantly. Some of the poignancy may come from the fact that she did not attain success herself, living as a virtual recluse in her father's house, never finding a response to love, scribbling her little poems on pieces of paper which were mostly published after her death. Here is a woman who seemingly had achieved nothing.

> Success is counted sweetest
> By those who ne'er succeed.
> To comprehend a nectar
> Requires sorest need.
>
> Not one of all the purple host
> Who took the flag to-day
> Can tell the definition,
> So clear, of victory,
>
> As he, defeated, dying,
> On whose forbidden ear
> The distant strains of triumph
> Burst agonized and clear!

The Voice

Thomas Hardy 1840–1928

I DO NOT think Thomas Hardy was the most balanced of men. His pessimism and his self-centredness often annoy me, yet there is real misery here. Hardy realized he loved his first wife only after she died. He was a young architect who married into a family of a slightly higher social status. It is not just that he missed his wife after her death, but that he had always 'missed' her when she was alive, for he neglected her shamefully. Only after her death was he able to feel the full failure of his marriage. At the end of the poem, where he says, 'thus I; faltering forward, Leaves around me falling', we feel the change of tempo: he becomes more self-aware and allows his emotions to overcome him.

Woman much missed, how you call to me, call to me,
Saying that now you are not as you were
When you had changed from the one who was all
    to me,
But as at first, when our day was fair.

Can it be you that I hear? Let me view you, then,
Standing as when I drew near to the town
Where you would wait for me: yes, as I knew you
    then,
Even to the original air-blue gown!

Or is it only the breeze, in its listlessness
Travelling across the wet mead to me here,
You being ever dissolved to wan wistlessness,
Heard no more again far or near?

   Thus I; faltering forward,
   Leaves around me falling,
Wind oozing thin through the thorn from norward,
   And the woman calling.

———— ❖❖❖ ————

Snake

D. H. Lawrence 1885–1930

SURELY it is a deep sorrow to know that in life a chance was offered, but that you spoiled it because you were petty. Lawrence, in his profound sympathy with the animal world, knew that his encounter with the snake ennobled him, lifted him up into something beautiful. Then he destroyed it through his own paltriness. As with prayer, the nearer you get to God, the more aware you are of any shabby behaviour, noticing things in yourself you would rather not have recognized. Only a man of Lawrence's spiritual capacity would realize that he had failed to live up to the snake.

A snake came to my water-trough
On a hot, hot day, and I in pyjamas for the heat,
To drink there.

In the deep, strange-scented shade of the great dark
        carob tree
I came down the steps with my pitcher
And must wait, must stand and wait, for there he was
        at the trough before me.

He reached down from a fissure in the earth-wall in
        the gloom
And trailed his yellow-brown slackness soft-bellied
        down, over the edge of the stone trough
And rested his throat upon the stone bottom,
And where the water had dripped from the tap, in a
        small clearness,
He sipped with his straight mouth,
Softly drank through his straight gums, into his slack
        long body,
Silently.

Someone was before me at my water-trough,
And I, like a second-comer, waiting.

He lifted his head from his drinking, as cattle do,
And looked at me vaguely, as drinking cattle do,
And flickered his two-forked tongue from his lips,
        and mused a moment,

101

And stooped and drank a little more,
Being earth-brown, earth-golden from the burning
       bowels of the earth
On the day of Sicilian July, with Etna smoking.

The voice of my education said to me
He must be killed,
For in Sicily the black, black snakes are innocent, the
       gold are venomous.

And voices in me said, If you were a man
You would take a stick and break him now, and finish
       him off.

But must I confess how I liked him,
How glad I was he had come like a guest in quiet, to
       drink at my water-trough
And depart peaceful, pacified, and thankless,
Into the burning bowels of this earth?

Was it cowardice, that I dared not kill him?
Was it perversity, that I longed to talk to him?
Was it humility, to feel so honoured?
I felt so honoured.

And yet those voices:
If you were not afraid, you would kill him!

And truly I was afraid, I was most afraid,
But even so, honoured still more
That he should seek my hospitality
From out the dark door of the secret earth.

He drank enough
And lifted his head, dreamily, as one who has
        drunken,
And flickered his tongue like a forked night on the
        air, so black,
Seeming to lick his lips,
And looked around like a god, unseeing, into the air,
And slowly turned his head,
And slowly, very slowly, as if thrice adream,
Proceeded to draw his slow length curving round
And climb again the broken bank of my wall-face.

And as he put his head into that dreadful hole,
And as he slowly drew up, snake-easing his shoulders,
        and entered farther,
A sort of horror, a sort of protest against his
        withdrawing into that horrid black hole,
Deliberately going into the blackness, and slowly
        drawing himself after,
Overcame me now his back was turned.

I looked round, I put down my pitcher,
I picked up a clumsy log
And threw it at the water-trough with a clatter.

I think it did not hit him,
But suddenly that part of him that was left behind
      convulsed in undignified haste,
Writhed like lightning, and was gone
Into the black hole, the earth-lipped fissure in the
      wallfront,
At which, in the intense still noon, I stared with
      fascination.

And immediately I regretted it.
I thought how paltry, how vulgar, what a mean act!
I despised myself and the voices of my accursed
      human education.

And I thought of the albatross,
And I wished he would come back, my snake.

For he seemed to me again like a king,
Like a king in exile, uncrowned in the underworld,
Now due to be crowned again.

And so, I missed my chance with one of the lords
Of life.
And I have something to expiate:
A pettiness.

To Daffadills

Robert Herrick 1591–1674

FOR SOME PEOPLE, the greatest of sorrows is the passing
of time, the shortness of life and the inability to hold
on to beauty. A life may bring fulfilment but it will also
bring sorrow. This is a very lyrical and gentle expression of
the great imposition laid on us. We live in time and have to
die. We cannot escape into a temporal vacuum.

> Faire Daffadills, we weep to see
> You haste away so soone:
> As yet the early-rising Sun
> Has not attain'd his Noone.
> Stay, stay,
> Until the hasting day
> Has run
> But to the Even-song;
> And, having pray'd together, we
> Will goe with you along.
>
> We have short time to stay, as you,
> We have as short a Spring;
> As quick a growth to meet Decay,
> As you, or any thing.
> We die,
> As your hours doe, and drie
> Away,
> Like to the Summeres raine;
> Or as the pearles of Mornings dew,
> Ne'er to be found again.

Binsey Poplars, Felled 1879

Gerard Manley Hopkins 1844–89

SOME OF THE poems in this section are grieving over things particular to the poet, but this one is more general. Hopkins laments our human capacity to destroy and even in its music the poetry is a dirge, 'All felled, felled, are all felled' – like a bell tolling 'Rural scene, a rural scene, Sweet especial rural scene', fading away from us. The poem holds a universal truth: we are perpetually destroying, even in innocence, not realizing what we do.

My aspens dear, whose airy cages quelled,
Quelled or quenched in leaves the leaping sun,
All felled, felled, are all felled;
   Of a fresh and following folded rank
       Not spared, not one
       That dandled a sandalled
     Shadow that swam or sank
On meadow and river and wind-wandering
    weed-winding bank.

O if we but knew what we do
    When we delve or hew –
   Hack and rack the growing green!
    Since country is so tender
   To touch, her being so slender,
   That, like this sleek and seeing ball
   But a prick will make no eye at all,

Where we, even when we mean
To mend her we end her,
When we hew or delve:
After-comers cannot guess the beauty been.
Ten or twelve, only ten or twelve
Strokes of havoc unselve
The sweet especial scene,
Rural scene, a rural scene,
Sweet especial rural scene.

———— ❖❖❖ ————

Dover Beach

Matthew Arnold 1820–88

ARNOLD IS TORN between a loss of faith and a grieving for faith (that suggests he still wants to believe). He desperately wants religion to be true and yet is desperately certain that it is not. In the last stanza we feel that whatever he would prefer he too has lost faith and is reduced to the bare conviction that the only protection he has against despair and misery comes from human relationships: 'Ah, love, let us be true to one another.'

The sea is calm to-night,
The tide is full, the moon lies fair
Upon the Straits;– on the French coast, the light
Gleams, and is gone; the cliffs of England stand,
Glimmering and vast, out in the tranquil bay.
Come to the window, sweet is the night air!
    Only, from the long line of spray
Where the ebb meets the moon-blanch'd land.
Listen! you hear the grating roar
Of pebbles which the waves suck back, and fling,
At their return, up the high strand,
Begin, and cease, and then again begin,
With tremulous cadence slow, and bring
The eternal note of sadness in.

    Sophocles long ago
Heard it on the Aegean, and it brought
Into his mind the turbid ebb and flow
    Of human misery; we
Find also in the sound a thought,
Hearing it by this distant northern sea.
    The sea of faith
Was once, too, at the full, and round earth's shore
Lay like the folds of a bright girdle furled;
    But now I only hear
Its melancholy, long, withdrawing roar,
    Retreating to the breath
Of the night-wind down the vast edges drear
And naked shingles of the world.

Ah, love, let us be true
To one another! for the world, which seems
To lie before us like a land of dreams,
So various, so beautiful, so new,
Hath really neither joy, nor love, nor light,
Nor certitude, nor peace, nor help for pain;
And we are here as on a darkling plain
Swept with confused alarms of struggle and flight,
Where ignorant armies clash by night.

———— ❖❖❖ ————

The Castaway
William Cowper 1731–1800

THIS POEM IS so powerful, because it is not merely a description of a drowning sailor, but a portrait of the poet's identification with the drowning man. The poet is intensely aware of cruelty, bitterness and desertion.

William Cowper suffered from two severe afflictions: he was an incurable depressive and he was a devout Nonconformist who believed in predestination. He could never feel that he was redeemed and so concluded that he was damned. Nothing could shake him from this belief. He had friends, but they had failed to check the vessel's course – the movement of his soul towards hellfire. Belief in predestination must have caused many a heart to break. The poem is so very moving because of its personal significance, which Cowper admits only in the last three lines.

Obscurest night involved the sky,
   The Atlantic billows roared,
When such a destined wretch as I,
   Washed headlong from on board,
Of friends, of hope, of all bereft,
His floating home for ever left.

No braver chief could Albion boast
   Than he with whom he went,
Nor ever ship left Albion's coast,
   With warmer wishes sent.
He loved them both, but both in vain,
Nor him beheld, nor her again.

Not long beneath the whelming brine,
   Expert to swim, he lay;
Nor soon he felt his strength decline,
   Or courage die away;
But waged with death a lasting strife,
Supported by despair of life.

He shouted: nor his friends had failed
   To check the vessel's course,
But so the furious blast prevailed,
   That, pitiless perforce,
They left their outcast mate behind,
And scudded still before the wind.

Some succour yet they could afford;
   And, such as storms allow,
The cask, the coop, the floated cord,
   Delayed not to bestow.
But he (they knew) nor ship, nor shore,
Whate'er they gave, should visit more.

Nor, cruel as it seemed, could he
   Their haste himself condemn,
Aware that flight, in such a sea,
   Alone could rescue them;
Yet bitter felt it still to dïe
Deserted, and his friends so nigh.

He long survives, who lives an hour
   In ocean, self-upheld;
And so long he, with unspent power,
   His destiny repelled;
And ever, as the minutes flew,
Entreated help, or cried – Adieu!

At length, his transient respite past,
   His comrades, who before
Had heard his voice in every blast,
   Could catch the sound no more.
For then, by toil subdued, he drank
The stifling wave, and then he sank.

No poet wept him: but the page
    Of narrative sincere,
That tells his name, his worth, his age,
    Is wet with Anson's tear.
And tears by bards or heroes shed
Alike immortalize the dead.

I therefore purpose not, or dream,
    Descanting on his fate,
To give the melancholy theme
    A more enduring date:
But misery still delights to trace
Its semblance in another's case.

No voice divine the storm allayed,
    No light propitious shone;
When, snatched from all effectual aid,
    We perished, each alone:
But I beneath a rougher sea,
And whelmed in deeper gulfs than he.

'So we'll go no more a-roving'

Lord Byron 1788–1824

BYRON REGRETS a lost youth. He still wants that youthful freedom, but can no longer stand up to its demands, both physical and emotional. It is a very reluctant admission that we cannot have everything and I think that we become mature only when we fully understand that, because it is in our nature to want everything. This is almost excessively true of Byron. It has to be forced upon us that human beings are finite and have, as he says, to 'pause', to 'rest' or they will 'wear out'.

So we'll go no more a-roving
    So late into the night,
Though the heart be still as loving,
    And the moon be still as bright.

For the sword outwears the sheath,
    And the soul wears out the breast,
And the heart must pause to breathe,
    And Love itself have rest.

Though the night was made for loving,
    And the day returns too soon,
Yet we'll go no more a-roving
    By the light of the moon.

FAITH

I N THE RELIGIOUS sense, faith is that essential virtue that enables us to cling with trust and love to that which we cannot see and of which we can never have material proof. It is a virtue so deep and all-encompassing that I find it difficult to write about. Those who belong to a religion will understand both my reticence and my gratitude for such a gift. However, the religious meaning is by no means the only significance in our lives of faith. There may not be other occasions when there is such an absolute absence of proof, but we meet at every turn occasions for human faith. So many aspects of our lives do not fall under our own control. To a certain extent we must take our teachers, our doctors, our lawyers, our governing bodies on faith. We must have faith in the untried potential of our own children, because unless they feel we believe in them, they may be damaged in their progress. All the poems here show different aspects of this beautiful quality and in their difference show its necessity and ubiquity.

Instructions

Sheri Hostetler

THIS IS THE declaration of a Mennonite, but it might be that of a Zen Buddhist. Any Christians startled by the injunction to give up God need to follow through Hostetler's thought: it is the idea of God, the constriction of concept, that we are asked to surrender until, austere and purified, we are free from all that does not matter.

> Give up the world; give up self; finally, give up God.
> Find god in rhododendrons and rocks,
> passers-by, your cat.
> Pare your beliefs, your absolutes.
> Make it simple; make it clean.
> No carry-on luggage allowed.
> Examine all you have
> with a loving and critical eye, then
> throw away some more.
> Repeat. Repeat.
> Keep this and only this:
> what your heart beats loudly for
> what feels heavy and full in your gut.
> There will only be one or two
> things you will keep,
> and they will fit lightly
> in your pocket.

Via Negativa

R. S. Thomas 1913–2000

ONE OF MY DEEPEST convictions is that God is a reality so absolute that all our other realities are relative. God so transcends all human conceptions that we can really only speak of him by way of negatives. We cannot see him, hear him, feel him, however ardently we long to. This is a poem about that enormous, bottomless space in our lives that God fills invisibly and inaudibly.

> Why no! I never thought other than
> That God is that great absence
> In our lives, the empty silence
> Within, the place where we go
> Seeking, not in hope to
> Arrive or find. He keeps the interstices
> In our knowledge, the darkness
> Between stars. His are the echoes
> We follow, the footprints he has just
> Left. We put our hands in
> His side hoping to find
> It warm. We look at people
> And places as though he had looked
> At them, too; but miss the reflection.

Love

George Herbert 1593–1633

I LIKE TO THINK of George Herbert, retired in his country rectory, physically in decline from what was probably consumption, but using his time with such love and devotion. 'Love' refers both to the Eucharistic Service and to the Marriage Feast of Heaven. There has never been a more tender evocation of God's love for us and his total forgiveness of our sinfulness. One knows, without needing to be told, that Herbert is speaking from personal experience.

> Love bade me welcome; yet my soul drew back,
>> Guilty of dust and sin.
> But quick-eyed Love, observing me grow slack
>> From my first entrance in,
> Drew nearer to me, sweetly questioning,
>> If I lacked any thing.
>
> 'A guest', I answered, 'worthy to be here.'
>> Love said, 'You shall be he.'
> 'I, the unkind, ungrateful? Ah, my dear,
>> I cannot look on thee.'
> Love took my hand, and smiling did reply,
>> 'Who made the eyes but I?'

'Truth, Lord, but I have marred them; let my shame
          Go where it doth deserve.'
'And know you not', says Love, 'who bore the blame?'
          'My dear, then I will serve.'
'You must sit down', says Love, 'and taste my meat.'
          So I did sit and eat.

———— ❖❖❖ ————

A Broken Image

Thomas Blackburn 1916–77

THIS IS A VERY clever poem, starting with the friendli-
ness of the anecdote and leading us imperceptibly on
to that silent, inexplicable, dark contact with God.

> Walking in the Alps, my wife and I
> Found a broken cross, half buried under
> A fall of rock and turf and red scree.
>
> Since it came away, the figure
> Of Christ, easily from its rusted
> Nail, under a worm-eaten, weather
>
> Worn image of wood we transported
> From Italy without permission
> We drink our wine now, eat our daily bread.

Since friends who come here often mention
The great skill of an anonymous
Carver of beech-wood, the conversation

Is enriched by his being with us
As at Cana, I'd say, if the bowed head
With any locality or surface

Chatter could be associated.
Leaning forward, as it does, from our wall
To where silence is concentrated

Outside and within the ephemeral
Constellations of energy,
Because it says nothing reasonable,

This image explains nothing away,
And just by gazing into darkness
Is able to mean more than words can say.

Lycidas

John Milton 1608–74

'LYCIDAS' HAS gone with me throughout my life. I used to know the whole poem by heart and at a pinch still do. Although I am embarrassed by the length, far outstripping that of every other poem in the anthology, in every section there are passages so dear to me that I feel it would be a true mutilation to cut it. Even the dark passages, when he is railing against the seventeenth-century church ('the hungry sheep look up and are not fed') I cannot bring myself to cut. In fact, dear Reader, if you were here and asked me to read you one poem from this collection, I'd ask you to put your feet up and listen to 'Lycidas'.

Yet once more, O ye laurels, and once more
Ye myrtles brown, with ivy never sere,
I come to pluck your berries harsh and crude,
And with forced fingers rude,
Shatter your leaves before the mellowing year.
Bitter constraint, and sad occasion dear,
Compels me to disturb your season due:
For Lycidas is dead, dead ere his prime,
Young Lycidas, and hath not left his peer:
Who would not sing for Lycidas? he knew
Himself to sing, and build the lofty rhyme.
He must not float upon his watery bier
Unwept, and welter to the parching wind,
Without the meed of some melodious tear.

Begin then, sisters of the sacred well,
That from beneath the seat of Jove doth spring,
Begin, and somewhat loudly sweep the string.
Hence with denial vain, and coy excuse,
So may some gentle muse
With lucky words favour my destined urn,
And as he passes turn,
And bid fair peace be to my sable shroud.
For we were nursed upon the self-same hill,
Fed the same flock; by fountain, shade, and rill.

Together both, ere the high lawns appeared
Under the opening eye-lids of the morn,
We drove a-field, and both together heard
What time the grey-fly winds her sultry horn,
Battening our flocks with the fresh dews of night,
Oft till the star that rose, at evening, bright,
Toward heaven's descent had sloped his westering
    wheel.
Meanwhile the rural ditties were not mute,
Tempered to the oaten flute,
Rough satyrs danced, and fauns with cloven heel,
From the glad sound would not be absent long,
And old Damaetas loved to hear our song.

But O the heavy change, now thou art gone,
Now thou art gone, and never must return!
Thee shepherd, thee the woods, and desert caves,
With wild thyme and the gadding vine o'ergrown,
And all their echoes mourn.
The willows, and the hazel copses green,

Shall now no more be seen,
Fanning their joyous leaves to thy soft lays.
As killing as the canker to the rose,
Or taint-worm to the weanling herds that graze,
Or frost to flowers, that their gay wardrobe wear,
When first the white-thorn blows;
Such, Lycidas, thy loss to shepherd's ear.
   Where were ye nymphs when the remorseless deep
Closed o'er the head of your loved Lycidas?
For neither were ye playing on the steep,
Where your old bards, the famous Druids, lie,
Nor on the shaggy top of Mona high,
Nor yet where Deva spreads her wizard stream:
Ay me, I fondly dream!
Had ye been there … for what could that have done?
What could the muse herself that Orpheus bore,
The muse herself for her enchanting son
Whom universal nature did lament,
When by the rout that made the hideous roar,
His gory visage down the stream was sent,
Down the swift Hebrus to the Lesbian shore.
   Alas! What boots it with uncessant care
To tend the homely slighted shepherd's trade,
And strictly meditate the thankless muse,
Were it not better done as others use,
To sport with Amaryllis in the shade,
Or with the tangles of Neaera's hair?
Fame is the spur that the clear spirit doth raise
(That last infirmity of noble mind)

To scorn delights, and live laborious days;
But the fair guerdon when we hope to find,
And think to burst out into sudden blaze,
Comes the blind Fury with th' abhorred shears,
And slits the thin-spun life. But not the praise,
Phoebus replied, and touched my trembling ears;
Fame is no plant that grows on mortal soil,
Nor in the glistering foil
Set off to the world, nor in broad rumour lies,
But lives and spreads aloft by those pure eyes,
And perfect witness of all-judging Jove;
As he pronounces lastly on each deed,
Of so much fame in heaven expect thy meed.

O fountain Arethuse, and thou honoured flood,
Smooth-sliding Mincius, crowned with vocal reeds,
That strain I heard was of a higher mood:
But now my oat proceeds,
And listens to the herald of the sea
That came in Neptune's plea,
He asked the waves, and asked the felon winds,
What hard mishap hath doomed this gentle swain?
And questioned every gust of rugged wings
That blows from off each beaked promontory:
They knew not of his story,
And sage Hippotades their answer brings,
That not a blast was from his dungeon strayed,
The air was calm, and on the level brine,
Sleek Panope with all her sisters played.
It was that fatal and perfidious bark

Built in the eclipsé, and rigged with curses dark,
That sunk so low that sacred head of thine.
   Next Camus, reverend sire, went footing slow,
His mantle hairy, and his bonnet sedge,
Inwrought with figures dim, and on the edge
Like to that sanguine flower inscribed with woe.
Ah; who hath reft (quoth he) my dearest pledge?
Last came, and last did go,
The pilot of the Galilean lake,
Two massy keys he bore of metals twain,
(The golden opes, the iron shuts amain)
He shook his mitred locks, and stern bespake,
How well could I have spared for thee, young swain,
Enow of such as for their bellies' sake,
Creep and intrude, and climb into the fold?
Of other care they little reckoning make,
Than how to scramble at the shearers' feast,
And shove away the worthy bidden guest;
Blind mouths! that scarce themselves know how
      to hold
A sheep-hook, or have learned aught else the least
That to the faithful herdman's art belongs!
What recks it them? What need they? They are sped;
And when they list, their lean and flashy songs
Grate on their scrannel pipes of wretched straw,
The hungry sheep look up, and are not fed,
But swoll'n with wind, and the rank mist they draw,
Rot inwardly, and foul contagion spread:
Besides what the grim wolf with privy paw

Daily devours apace, and nothing said,
But that two-handed engine at the door,
Stands ready to smite once, and smite no more.
　　Return Alpheus, the dread voice is past,
That shrunk thy steams; return Sicilian muse,
And call the vales, and bid them hither cast
Their bells, and flowrets of a thousand hues.
Ye valleys low where the mild whispers use,
Of shades and wanton winds, and gushing brooks,
On whose fresh lap the swart star sparely looks,
Throw hither all your quaint enamelled eyes,
That on the green turf suck the honied showers,
And purple all the ground with vernal flowers.
Bring the rathe primrose that forsaken dies,
The tufted crow-toe, and pale jessamine,
The white pink, and the pansy freaked with jet,
The glowing violet
The musk-rose, and the well-attired woodbine,
With cowslips wan that hang the pensive head,
And every flower that sad embroidery wears:
Bid amaranthus all his beauty shed,
And daffadillies fill their cups with tears,
To strew the laureate hearse where Lycid lies.
For so to interpose a little ease,
Let our frail thoughts dally with false surmise.
Ay me! Whilst thee the shores, and sounding seas
Wash far away where'er thy bones are hurled,
Whether beyond the stormy Hebrides
Where thou perhaps under the whelming tide

Visit'st the bottom of the monstrous world;
Or whether thou to our moist vows denied.
Sleep'st by the fable of Bellerus old,
Where the great vision of the guarded mount
Looks toward Namancos and Bayona's hold;
Look homeward angel now, and melt with ruth.
And, O ye dolphins, waft the hapless youth.

    Weep no more, woeful shepherds weep no more
For Lycidas your sorrow is not dead,
Sunk though he be beneath the watery floor,
So sinks the day-star in the ocean bed,
And yet anon repairs his drooping head,
And tricks his beams, and with new spangled ore,
Flames in the forehead of the morning sky:
So Lycidas sunk low, but mounted high,
Through the dear might of him that walked the
       waves;
Where other groves, and other streams along,
With nectar pure his oozy locks he laves,
And hears the unexpressive nuptial song,
In the blest kingdoms meek of joy and love.
There entertain him all the saints above,
In solemn troops, and sweet societies
That sing, and singing in their glory move,
And wipe the tears for ever from his eyes.
Now, Lycidas, the shepherds weep no more;
Henceforth thou art the genius of the shore,
In thy large recompense, and shalt be good
To all that wander in that perilous flood.

Thus sang the uncouth swain to the oaks and rills,
While the still morn went out with sandals grey
He touched the tender stops of various quills,
With eager thought warbling his Doric lay:
And now the sun had stretched out all the hills,
And now was dropped into the western bay;
At last he rose, and twitched his mantle blue:
Tomorrow to fresh woods, and pastures new.

———— ❖❖❖ ————

Nativity Poem

Joseph Brodsky 1940–96

Translated by Seamus Heaney

ANYONE WHO HAS attended Midnight Mass at Christmas or seen the Christmas crib will respond to what Brodsky is seeking to draw from us. Seven times in the poem he calls on us to 'imagine' and, benevolent poet that he is, provides us with all the evocative sights, sounds, even images of touch that will help us to enter into this essentially unimaginable event.

Imagine striking a match that night in the cave:
Imagine crockery, try to make use of its glaze
To feel cold cracks in the floor, the blankness of
        hunger.
Imagine the desert – but the desert is everywhere.

Imagine striking a match in that midnight cave,
The fire, the farm beasts in outline, the farm tools
        and stuff;
And imagine, as you towel your face in enveloping
        folds,
Mary, Joseph, and the Infant in swaddling clothes.

Imagine the kings, the caravans' stilted procession
As they make for the cave, or, rather, three beams
        closing in
And in on the star; the creaking of loads, the clink
        of a cowbell;
(No thronging of Heaven as yet, no peal of the bell

That will ring in the end for the Infant once he has
        earned it).
Imagine the Lord, for the first time, from darkness,
        and stranded
Immensely in distance, recognizing Himself in
        the Son
Of Man: His homelessness plain to him now in a
        homeless one.

'anyone lived in a pretty how town'

e. e. cummings 1894–1962

FAITH IS NOT necessarily Faith in God, although that is how we think of it, with a capital 'F'. But there can be secular forms. (We say 'I have faith in you'.) Here, there is faith in the everlasting rhythm of human life, seemingly inconsequential and forgotten. Cummings's playful way with words emphasizes that it is not the specific he is concerned with here, but the general: the vast mass of humanity living their quiet lives, dying, and their children taking up the pattern. This is a good instance of how a poem is not written with ideas, which may be clichéd, but with words, the arrangement and music of which make poetry.

anyone lived in a pretty how town
(with up so floating many bells down)
spring summer autumn winter
he sang his didn't he danced his did.

Women and men (both little and small)
cared for anyone not at all
they sowed their isn't they reaped their same
sun moon stars rain
children guessed (but only a few
and down they forgot as up they grew
autumn winter spring summer)
that noone loved him more by more

when by now and tree by leaf
she laughed his joy she cried his grief
bird by snow and stir by still
anyone's any was all to her

someones married their everyones
laughed their cryings and did their dance
(sleep wake hope and then) they
said their nevers they slept their dream

stars rain sun moon
(and only the snow can begin to explain
how children are apt to forget to remember
with up so floating many bells down)

one day anyone died i guess
(and noone stooped to kiss his face)
busy folk buried them side by side
little by little and was by was

all by all and deep by deep
and more by more they dream their sleep
noone and anyone earth by april
wish by spirit and if by yes.

Women and men (both dong and ding)
summer autumn winter spring
reaped their sowing and went their came
sun moon stars rain

Jerome

Gabriel Levin b. 1948

I AM FREQUENTLY amazed at how often the Old Masters painted St Jerome. They saw him from two aspects, almost contradictory. One image is of the naked Jerome in the desert, beating his breast with a stone, cardinal's hat thrown on to a nearby rock, lion snuffling supportively in the background. This is Jerome the penitent. The other image, equally frequent, is of Jerome the scholar and here Levin has in mind the extraordinary painting in the National Gallery in London. He sees this painting not only for what it is, a marvellous image of a Renaissance study, but for what it implies about Jerome's faith and his labours in translating the Bible – would-be food for a world that believed in God but could not read Hebrew.

Walled in by the desert, he had no patience
for the solitary rigours of monks in rags
and, notwithstanding the brushwork of pinched
flesh-tints (the wasting away and slag
of self-immolation) displayed on canvas and panel,
the barometer of his affections drew him
elsewhere and turned him into a pupil
of Hebrew, "this language of hissing and grim
aspirates". But I see him as Antonello
da Messina – who brought to Venice the secrets
of oil glazing – saw him: in the airiness
of his study, where the play of light mellows

chapter and verse, propped on his desk,
on which he trains his mind in muted bliss.
– He who'd pleaded, "Step out, I beg you, a little
from your body," scrapes back his chair
and treads three steps down, while the peaceable
lion pads in the cloister with nowhere
to go, lost in a perspective that fools the eye
and bids the heart to linger in the domed
mansion, at noon-tide, amid the cries
of swifts, glimpsed through the high windows,
seeding the air. To live and move
under the veritable Bethlehem skies, and *thrust
the hand into the flame* translating the Good
Book for everyman, and day by day to prove
how words might heave and break the crust,
the hard Judean soil, and serve as food.

---❖❖❖---

Bermudas

Andrew Marvell 1621–78

THIS IS ANOTHER poem I have loved since my Oxford days. Marvell's extraordinary awareness of the beauty of the world is here a vehicle to proclaim the glory of God. He imagines the early Nonconformists, forced by religious intolerance to leave their own country, glorifying God in the strangeness of their new home: the remote Bermudas. In a way it is a poem as much about courage as about faith.

Where the remote Bermudas ride,
In th' ocean's bosom unespied,
From a small boat that rowed along,
The listening winds received this song:
   'What should we do but sing His praise,
That led us through the watery maze
Unto an isle so long unknown,
And yet far kinder than our own?
Where He the huge sea monsters wracks,
That lift the deep upon their backs;
He lands us on a grassy stage,
Safe from the storms, and prelate's rage.
He gave us this eternal spring
Which here enamels everything,
And sends the fowls to us in care,
On daily visits through the air;
He hangs in shades the orange bright,
Like golden lamps in a green night,
And does in the pomegranates close
Jewels more rich than Ormus shows;
He makes the figs our mouths to meet,
And throws the melons at our feet;
But apples plants of such a price,
No tree could ever bear them twice;
With cedars, chosen by His hand,
From Lebanon, He stores the land;
And makes the hollow seas, that roar,
Proclaim the ambergris on shore;
He cast (of which we rather boast)

The Gospel's pearl upon our coast,
And in these rocks for us did frame
A temple, where to sound His name.
O! let our voice His praise exalt,
Till it arrive at heaven's vault,
Which, thence (perhaps) rebounding, may
Echo beyond the Mexique Bay.'

   Thus sung they in the English boat,
An holy and a cheerful note;
And all the way, to guide their chime,
With falling oars they kept the time.

HOPE

HOPE, LIKE FAITH, is one of the three theological virtues. Of the three it is perhaps the least noticed and appreciated (charity outshines it and faith bulks in front of it). Yet without hope we are doomed to misery. It is hope that gives us the certainty that all that we believe in as Christians or Muslims or Jews or whatever and all that we love will one day receive us into everlasting joy. We may not be fully aware of this certainty, but nevertheless it is our motor power. Here again the religious meaning is by no means exclusive. We *can* live on hopelessly, despairingly, refusing to admit even the possibility of a brighter prospect, but it is rare to find such determined masochism. Even the most hardened pessimist hopes that you will come to see the rightness of his opinions. We use hope freely in our conversation and in our literature too, because this desire for good things to come springs from the depth of our consciousness. Think of Noah and the Flood and the repeated despatch of a bird to assess whether the waters, which were all that Noah could see, had somewhere or somehow receded. We are incomplete if we are without a touch of that irrepressible hope. Fortunately too, since our hopes are often rather foolish, their failure does not depress us over much. We rise up and hope again.

Watching for Dolphins

David Constantine b.1944

HUMAN HOPE can be disappointed. It is important that we realize this: 'All, unaccustomed, wanted epiphany, Praying the sky ...', but life does not work like that. This is not a very short poem, but Constantine could not have written it more economically because here the length of the form contains the meaning. The expectation that the dolphins will appear builds up progressively, until we think the intensity of the emotion will make it happen.

In the summer months on every crossing to Piraeus
One noticed that certain passengers soon rose
From seats in the packed saloon and with serious
Looks and no acknowledgement of a common
     purpose
Passed forward through the small door into the bows
To watch for dolphins. One saw them lose

Every other wish. Even the lovers
Turned their desires on the sea, and a fat man
Hung with equipment to photograph the occasion
Stared like a saint, through sad bi-focals; others,
Hopeless themselves, looked to the children for they
Would see dolphins if anyone would. Day after day

Or on their last opportunity all gazed
Undecided whether a flat calm were favourable
Or a sea the sun and the wind between them raised
To a likeness of dolphins. Were gulls a sign, that fell
Screeching from the sky or over an unremarkable
      place
Sat in a silent school? Every face

After its character implored the sea.
All, unaccustomed, wanted epiphany,
Praying the sky would clang and the abused Aegean
Reverberate with cymbal, gong and drum.
We could not imagine more prayer, and had they then
On the waves, on the climax of our longing come

Smiling, snub-nosed, domed like satyrs, oh
We should have laughed and lifted the children up
Stranger to stranger, pointing how with a leap
They left their element, three or four times, centred
On grace, and heavily and warm re-entered,
Looping the keel. We should have felt them go

Further and further into the deep parts. But soon
We were among the great tankers, under their chains
In black water. We had not seen the dolphins
But woke, blinking. Eyes cast down
With no admission of disappointment the company
Dispersed and prepared to land in the city.

Church Going

Philip Larkin 1922–85

ALTHOUGH LARKIN portrays the Church as obsolete in the early stanzas, just being there gives him a sense of being in the right place, of fulfilling a need that any of us may, unexpectedly, experience at some stage. In its oblique way, this is a poem about hope.

Once I am sure there's nothing going on
I step inside, letting the door thud shut.
Another church: matting, seats, and stone,
And little books; sprawlings of flowers, cut
For Sunday, brownish now; some brass and stuff
Up at the holy end; the small neat organ;
And a tense, musty, unignorable silence,
Brewed God knows how long. Hatless, I take off
My cycle-clips in awkward reverence,

Move forward, run my hand around the font.
From where I stand, the roof looks almost new –
Cleaned, or restored? Someone would know: I don't.
Mounting the lectern, I peruse a few
Hectoring large-scale verses, and pronounce
'Here endeth' much more loudly than I'd meant.
The echoes snigger briefly. Back at the door
I sign the book, donate an Irish sixpence,
Reflect the place was not worth stopping for.

Yet stop I did: in fact I often do,
And always end much at a loss like this,
Wondering what to look for; wondering, too,
When churches fall completely out of use
What we shall turn them into, if we shall keep
A few cathedrals chronically on show,
Their parchment, plate and pyx in locked cases,
And let the rest rent-free to rain and sheep.
Shall we avoid them as unlucky places?

Or, after dark, will dubious women come
To make their children touch a particular stone;
Pick simples for a cancer; or on some
Advised night see walking a dead one?
Power of some sort or other will go on
In games, in riddles, seemingly at random;
But superstition, like belief, must die,
And what remains when disbelief has gone?
Grass, weedy pavement, brambles, buttress, sky,

A shape less recognisable each week,
A purpose more obscure. I wonder who
Will be the last, the very last, to seek
This place for what it was; one of the crew
That tap and jot and know what rood-lofts were?
Some ruin-bibber, randy for antique,
Or Christmas-addict, counting on a whiff
Of gown-and-bands and organ-pipes and myrrh?
Or will he be my representative,

Bored, uninformed, knowing the ghostly silt
Dispersed, yet tending to this cross of ground
Through suburb scrub because it held unspilt
So long and equably what since is found
Only in separation – marriage, and birth,
And death, and thoughts of these – for which was built
This special shell? For, though I've no idea
What this accoutred frowsty barn is worth,
It pleases me to stand in silence here;

A serious house on serious earth it is,
In whose blent air all our compulsions meet,
Are recognised, and robed as destinies.
And that much never can be obsolete,
Since someone will forever be surprising
A hunger in himself to be more serious,
And gravitating with it to this ground,
Which, he once heard, was proper to grow wise in,
If only that so many dead lie round.

Hymn to Diana

Ben Jonson 1572–1637

AGAIN, THIS poem is not about Christian hope, but about a hope that prayer can bring blessings. Jonson asks for the ability to see and he asks for spiritual space. Why pray at all, unless you have hope of an answer?

> Queen and huntress, chaste and fair,
>   Now the sun is laid to sleep,
> Seated in thy silver chair,
>   State in wonted manner keep:
>   Hesperus entreats thy light,
>   Goddess excellently bright.

> Earth, let not thy envious shade
>   Dare itself to interpose;
> Cynthia's shining orb was made
>   Heaven to clear when day did close:
>   Bless us then with wishèd sight,
>   Goddess excellently bright.

> Lay thy bow of pearl apart,
>   And thy crystal-shining quiver;
> Give unto the flying hart
>   Space to breathe, how short soever:
>   Thou that mak'st a day of night–
>   Goddess excellently bright.

Eden Rock

Charles Causley 1917–2003

IT IS THE SWEET simplicity of this poem that so attracts me. It is almost as if the poet holds up an old photograph which recalls a memory and in the strange happiness of this encounter he begins, wonderingly, to understand death and its reunions.

> They are waiting for me somewhere beyond Eden
>   Rock:
> My father, twenty-five, in the same suit
> Of Genuine Irish Tweed, his terrier Jack
> Still two years old and trembling at his feet.
>
> My mother, twenty-three, in a sprigged dress
> Drawn at the waist, ribbon in her straw hat,
> Has spread the stiff white cloth over the grass.
> Her hair, the colour of wheat, takes on the light.
>
> She pours tea from a Thermos, the milk straight
> From an old H.P. sauce bottle, a screw
> Of paper for a cork; slowly sets out
> The same three plates, the tin cups painted blue.
>
> The sky whitens as if lit by three suns.
> My mother shades her eyes and looks my way
> Over the drifted stream. My father spins
> A stone along the water. Leisurely,

They beckon to me from the other bank.
I hear them call, 'See where the stream-path is!
Crossing is not as hard as you might think.'

I had not thought that it would be like this.

———— ❖❖❖ ————

The Darkling Thrush
Thomas Hardy 1840–1928

PART OF THE eerie fascination that Hardy holds for me is his intense interest in himself. This marvellous poem, however, springs from a wider concern: the misery of the times and the extraordinary rapture of the aged thrush. It is rare to find some 'blessed Hope' in Hardy and a great subject for rejoicing.

I leant upon a coppice gate
    When Frost was spectre-gray,
And Winter's dregs made desolate
    The weakening eye of day.
The tangled bine-stems scored the sky
    Like strings of broken lyres,
And all mankind that haunted nigh
    Had sought their household fires.

The land's sharp features seemed to be
   The Century's corpse outleant,
His crypt the cloudy canopy,
   The wind his death-lament.

The ancient pulse of germ and birth
   Was shrunken hard and dry,
And every spirit upon earth
   Seemed fervourless as I.

At once a voice arose among
   The bleak twigs overhead
In a full-hearted evensong
   Of joy illimited;
An aged thrush, frail, gaunt, and small,
   In blast-beruffled plume,
Had chosen thus to fling his soul
   Upon the growing gloom.

So little cause for carolings
   Of such ecstatic sound
Was written on terrestrial things
   Afar or nigh around,
That I could think there trembled through
   His happy goodnight air
Some blessed Hope, whereof he knew
   And I was unaware.

The Snow Village

Glyn Maxwell b. 1962

MAXWELL PLAYS with the idea of pen and paper and the mystery of being able to light up the page with knowledge: the snow in his image may erase all trace of a man's passage, but the nib will retain it. This is not as easy a poem as it first seems, but to me it is about the hope of communication.

In the age of pen and paper,
when the page was a snow village,
when days the light was leafing through
descended without message,

the nib that struck from heaven
was the sight of a cottage window
lit by the only certain
sign of a life, a candle,

glimpsed by a stranger walking
at a loss through the snow village.
All that can flow can follow
that sighting, though no image,

no face appear – not even
the hand that draws across it –
though the curtains close the vision,
though the stranger end his visit,

though the snow erase all traces
of his passing through the village,
though his step become unknowable
and the whiteness knowledge.

——— ❖❖❖ ———

'We had tired of confusion'
Roger Lipsey b. 1942

THIS POEM was sent to me by the author of a book on the writings of Thomas Merton (1915–68), an American monk who was an important figure in the post-war revival of interest in prayer. Merton's best-known book is *The Seven Storey Mountain*, but he wrote that early in his life as a monk. Towards the end, Merton became very interested in Zen Buddhism and I think the Zen-like experience that Lipsey communicates so well, of going up and coming down the mountain, and the discovery that his wife makes in their own garden, would have delighted that unusual Cistercian monk.

We had tired of confusion, stupidity, and evil
And so we climbed the mountain to see
From a great height, through clearest air,
The grand design. We saw the abstract
Of experience: the sacred algorithm
That shakes itself into ten thousand forms and lives,

Sets the swarm in motion though it is simple in itself,
Even slightly naïve.

We were dazzled. But my wife was soon uneasy.
'I miss *little* things,' she said. 'I can't see threads or bugs
Or harmless errors. I can't see second tries.
Can we go down the mountain just a bit?'

And so we turned from the source
And descended to a col at middle height
Where the view was narrower but scarcely less grand.
To our surprise we heard voices, wing beats,
Newborns wailing, leaves unfolding from moist stems,
Footsteps, breaths … And conspiracy, bloodshed, folly.
Light and dark mix there: the sacred algorithm hesitates,
Shivers like a doubting creature, and resumes its
        faithful plunge.

We were dazzled. But my wife was uneasy.
'I hear our niece weeping,' she said. 'We must go to her.'
And so we left the mountain and dined that evening
With our niece, who needed only kindness to smile
        again.
But I could not free myself from longing to return to
        the heights:
Like the faint scent of incense after a ceremony,
Memories of our expedition hung in the air. Until one
        day:

'Look,' she said – and held up to the light a tiny object.
'I found it this morning when I was planting green
        peas!'
It was a perfect replica of the sacred algorithm,
Pulsing with milky light, slightly naïve, entirely blessed.
'Shall we plant it?'

LOVE

———— ❖❖❖ ————

D O YOU REMEMBER St Paul on the virtues? 'And the greatest of these is love.' Some versions have it as 'charity', feeling perhaps that there is a certain ambiguity about love. Unfortunately there is also an ambiguity about charity, with its connotations of largesse handed out to the poor. The word I would most like to use, as I have suggested in the Introduction, is 'reverence'.

Moving away, though, from the religious context, a category of poems devoted to love has endless possibility for ambiguity and a satisfying complexity. If what springs to mind first is sexual love, that bliss for man and woman alike, think also of the tenderness of parental love, the flattering devotion of animal love (canine especially). There is love between friends, there is love for all that enhances the quality of our lives, whether books, games, wines or success in one endeavour or another. We love memories. We love our homes and our countries. As you can see, the potential list is endless.

Knowing love, giving and receiving it, is the most precious of experiences. Rare, perhaps non-existent, is the person who can come to the fullness of maturity without the surrender that is of the essence of love. Love abnegates itself gladly and in the abnegation receives more than is given. Pondering on the miraculous power of love, I have come to understand how the Scriptures can dare to say, 'God is love'.

Sonnet CXVI

William Shakespeare 1564–1616

IF 'LYCIDAS' IS the greatest long poem ever written, then this, I think, is the greatest sonnet. Not only are the words and music of it so beautiful, but the actual content (that love does not depend upon externals) is so marvellously true: 'Love is not love which alters when it alteration finds'. People know this best with their children, but it applies to all true love.

Let me not to the marriage of true minds
    Admit impediments. Love is not love
Which alters when it alteration finds,
    Or bends with the remover to remove.
O, no! it is an ever-fixèd mark,
    That looks on tempests and is never shaken;
It is the star to every wandering bark,
    Whose worth's unknown, although his height
      be taken.
Love's not Time's fool, though rosy lips and cheeks
    Within his bending sickle's compass come;
Love alters not with his brief hours and weeks,
    But bears it out even to the edge of doom.
      If this be error, and upon me proved,
      I never writ, nor no man ever loved.

Waking with Russell

Don Paterson b. 1963

MANY PEOPLE will respond to Paterson's experience: the almost ecstatic love a parent feels when a child is born. The poet takes it even further in a wonderful expression of the truth that you become young again through your child. The birth of Russell has changed his father: pitching back 'not my old hard-pressed grin but his own smile'.

Whatever the difference is, it all began
the day we woke up face-to-face like lovers
and his four-day-old smile dawned on him again,
possessed him, till it would not fall or waver;
and I pitched back not my old hard-pressed grin
but his own smile, or one I'd rediscovered.
Dear son, I was *mezzo del' cammin*
and the true path was as lost to me as ever
when you cut in front and lit it as you ran.
See how the true gift never leaves the giver:
returned and redelivered, it rolled on
until the smile poured through us like a river.
How fine, I thought, this waking amongst men!
I kissed your mouth and pledged myself forever.

'John Anderson my jo'

Robert Burns 1759–96

IMET THIS poem when I was a schoolchild and it has
stayed in my mind as the most beautiful description I
know of the happiness of marriage. Ironically, this was a
happiness which Burns himself was not to know.

> John Anderson my jo, John,
>   When we were first acquent,
> Your locks were like the raven,
>   Your bonnie brow was brent;
> But now your brow is beld, John,
>   Your locks are like the snow;
> But blessings on your frosty pow,
>   John Anderson, my jo.
>
> John Anderson my jo, John,
>   We clamb the hill thegither;
> And mony a canty day, John,
>   We've had wi' ane anither:
> Now we maun totter down, John,
>   And hand in hand we'll go,
> And sleep thegither at the foot,
>   John Anderson, my jo.

A Marriage

R. S. Thomas 1913–2000

THIS IS A LOVE poem called forth by death. Thomas muses on how quickly his marriage has passed, how almost without him noticing his wife's body has diminished to a bird-like frailty. The ending, 'one sigh no heavier than a feather', expresses for me the poem itself in its slightness and sadness, its grief and its love.

> We met
> under a shower
> of bird-notes.
> Fifty years passed,
> love's moment
> in a world in
> servitude to time.
> She was young;
> I kissed with my eyes
> closed and opened
> them on her wrinkles.
> 'Come,' said death,
> choosing her as his
> partner for
> the last dance. And she,
> who in life
> had done everything
> with a bird's grace,
> opened her bill now
> for the shedding
> of one sigh no
> heavier than a feather.

Swans Mating

Michael Longley b. 1939

HERE IS A wonderful example of the economy of poetry. In the first line Longley laments that his beloved is not with him, yet in the rest of the poem what he writes about the two swans is suffused with the presence of his absent wife.

> Even now I wish that you had been there
> Sitting beside me on the riverbank:
> The cob and his hen sailing in rhythm
> Until their small heads met and the final
> Heraldic moment dissolved in ripples.
>
> This was a marriage and a baptism,
> A holding of breath, nearly a drowning,
> Wings spread wide for balance where he trod,
> Her feathers full of water and her neck
> Under the water like a bar of light.

Feral

John Harris

IT WAS AUDEN, I think, who said that when we describe animals we describe ourselves. Whether it is true or not, nothing can diminish for me the pleasure I feel in this sensitive description of a semi-feral cat. I am particularly fond of cats – my favourite animal – and I sympathize equally with the poet, held at a distance by the cat who 'loves' but is unable to 'trust'.

> He loves me
> but doesn't trust me.
>
> His large green eyes
> regard me with suspicion –
> always.
>
> Hypersensitive –
> like so many damaged creatures –
> he feels my emotions
> before I do;
> reads my thoughts
> before they are formulated.
>
> He swiftly flows over the end
> of the mattress. Vanishes.

Later, he will
re-materialize in mid-air,

land weightlessly on the bed
and regard me from an unreachable
distance,

studying me for subtle signs,
more than a little interested
in affection;

poised for flight.

———— ❖❖❖ ————

Those Winter Sundays
Robert Hayden 1913–80

HAYDEN PUTS his finger on the type of love that adults often only realize when they become parents themselves. The father, with his cracked hands and daily labours, rises to serve the son, and the son, who has clearly outgrown his father (notice the good shoes), regards him with indifference. He looks back with a pang of sorrow at how he has ignored the humble efforts of his father's service.

Sundays too my father got up early
and put his clothes on in the blueblack cold,
then with cracked hands that ached
from labor in the weekday weather made
banked fires blaze. No one ever thanked him.

I'd wake and hear the cold splintering, breaking.
When the rooms were warm, he'd call,
and slowly I would rise and dress,
fearing the chronic angers of that house,

Speaking indifferently to him,
who had driven out the cold
and polished my good shoes as well.
What did I know, what did I know
of love's austere and lonely offices?

———— ❖❖❖ ————

'Since there's no help, come, let us kiss and part'
Michael Drayton 1563–1631

WE THINK we are reading a poem of forced jubilation over a failed love. We may suspect that Drayton is not as glad as he proclaims himself to be, but he reiterates that the love between them is utterly and completely over. Then, wittily and touchingly, in the very last line he reveals his secret hopes: he still loves and only needs a response for the affair to move blissfully 'from death to life'.

Since there's no help, come, let us kiss and part –
Nay, I have done: you get no more of me;
And I am glad, yea, glad with all my heart
That thus so cleanly I myself can free.
Shake hands forever, cancel all our vows,
And when we meet at any time again,
Be it not seen in either of our brows
That we one jot of former love retain.
Now at the last gasp of love's latest breath,
When, his pulse failing, Passion speechless lies,
When Faith is kneeling by his bed of death,
And Innocence is closing up his eyes, –
    Now, if thou wouldst, when all have given him over,
    From death to life thou mightst him yet recover.

Lullaby

W. H. Auden 1907–73

I THINK THIS poem is a moving expression of the
vulnerability of human love. Notice that the lover is
mortal and guilty and the poet is faithless. They are
flawed creatures but they love each other.

> Lay your sleeping head, my love,
> Human on my faithless arm;
> Time and fevers burn away
> Individual beauty from
> Thoughtful children, and the grave
> Proves the child ephemeral:
> But in my arms till break of day
> Let the living creature lie,
> Mortal, guilty, but to me
> The entirely beautiful.
>
> Soul and body have no bounds:
> To lovers as they lie upon
> Her tolerant enchanted slope
> In their ordinary swoon,
> Grave the vision Venus sends
> Of supernatural sympathy,
> Universal love and hope;
> While an abstract insight wakes
> Among the glaciers and the rocks
> The hermit's carnal ecstasy.

Certainty, fidelity
On the stroke of midnight pass
Like vibrations of a bell
And fashionable madmen raise
Their pedantic boring cry:
Every farthing of the cost,
All the dreaded cards foretell,
Shall be paid, but from this night
Not a whisper, not a thought,
Not a kiss nor look be lost.

Beauty, midnight, vision dies:
Let the winds of dawn that blow
Softly round your dreaming head
Such a day of welcome show
Eye and knocking heart may bless,
Find our mortal world enough;
Noons of dryness find you fed
By the involuntary powers,
Nights of insult let you pass
Watched by every human love.

A Birthday

Christina Rossetti 1830–94

THE PURITY OF the emotion carries with it rather excessive imagery. Her love, in this case, is Jesus. We are listening to Christina Rossetti at prayer.

> My heart is like a singing bird
>   Whose nest is in a watered shoot;
> My heart is like an apple tree
> Whose boughs are bent with thick-set fruit;
> My heart is like a rainbow shell
>   That paddles in a halcyon sea;
> My heart is gladder than all these,
>   Because my love is come to me.
>
> Raise me a dais of silk and down;
>   Hang it with vair and purple dyes;
> Carve it in doves and pomegranates,
>   And peacocks with a hundred eyes;
> Work it in gold and silver grapes,
>   In leaves, and silver fleurs-de-lys;
> Because the birthday of my life
>   Is come, my love is come to me.

Song

John Donne 1572–1631

DONNE ACKNOWLEDGES the anguish of having to leave his wife, but turns it into an expression of even greater love. His journey through love was turbulent, in that his wife's wealthy father disinherited her and cast her off because he did not think Donne, who was a rather lowly cleric at the time, was worthy of her.

> Sweetest love, I do not go
>   For weariness of thee,
> Nor in hope the world can show
>   A fitter love for me;
>   But since that I
> Must die at last, 'tis best
> To use myself in jest
>   Thus by fained deaths to die.
>
> Yesternight the sun went hence,
>   And yet is here today,
> He hath no desire nor sense,
>   Nor half so short a way:
>   Then fear not me,
> But believe that I shall make
> Speedier journeys, since I take
>   More wings and spurs than he.

An Arundel Tomb

Philip Larkin 1922–85

WHAT I ESPECIALLY love is Larkin's mastery of the nuance. The stone knight on the tomb is holding his lady's hand and the poet comments on the irony that this seems to be a great image of fidelity although it may not ever have had that meaning. Yet because the image exists it does indeed blazon forth true love: 'The stone fidelity they hardly meant has come to be.' Since love is a complex thing, it is right that we do not get a simplified celebration of it.

> Side by side, their faces blurred,
> The earl and countess lie in stone,
> Their proper habits vaguely shown
> As jointed armour, stiffened pleat,
> And that faint hint of the absurd –
> The little dogs under their feet.
>
> Such plainness of the pre-baroque
> Hardly involves the eye, until
> It meets his left-hand gauntlet, still
> Clasped empty in the other; and
> One sees, with a sharp tender shock,
> His hand withdrawn, holding her hand.

They would not think to lie so long.
Such faithfulness in effigy
Was just a detail friends would see:
A sculptor's sweet commissioned grace
Thrown off in helping to prolong
The Latin names around the base.

They would not guess how early in
Their supine stationary voyage
The air would change to soundless damage,
Turn the old tenantry away;
How soon succeeding eyes begin
To look, not read. Rigidly they

Persisted, linked, through lengths and breadths
Of time. Snow fell, undated. Light
Each summer thronged the glass. A bright
Litter of birdcalls strewed the same
Bone-riddled ground. And up the paths
The endless altered people came,

Washing at their identity.
Now, helpless in the hollow of
An unarmorial age, a trough
Of smoke in slow suspended skeins
Above their scrap of history,
Only an attitude remains:

Time has transfigured them into
Untruth. The stone fidelity
They hardly meant has come to be
Their final blazon, and to prove
Our almost-instinct almost true:
What will survive of us is love.

———— ❖❖❖ ————

Meeting Point

Louis MacNeice 1907–63

I LOVE THIS poem for the world and the emotions that it conjures up. I have always been struck that not until the sixth stanza do we realize that it is the man who has been speaking. Up until then they do not really divide into two people. I have been told that the setting in the café and the meeting of the 'two people with one pulse' recalls the film *Brief Encounter*.

Time was away and somewhere else,
There were two glasses and two chairs
And two people with the one pulse
(Somebody stopped the moving stairs):
Time was away and somewhere else.

And they were neither up nor down;
The stream's music did not stop
Flowing through heather, limpid brown,
Although they sat in a coffee shop
And they were neither up nor down.

The bell was silent in the air
Holding its inverted poise –
Between the clang and clang a flower,
A brazen calyx of no noise:
The bell was silent in the air.

The camels crossed the miles of sand
That stretched around the cups and plates;
The desert was their own, they planned
To portion out the stars and dates:
The camels crossed the miles of sand.

Time was away and somewhere else.
The waiter did not come, the clock
Forgot them and the radio waltz
Came out like water from a rock:
Time was away and somewhere else.

Her fingers flicked away the ash
That bloomed again in tropic trees:
Not caring if the markets crash
When they had forests such as these,
Her fingers flicked away the ash.

God or whatever means the Good
Be praised that time can stop like this,
That what the heart has understood
Can verify in the body's peace
God or whatever means the Good.

Time was away and she was here
And life no longer what it was,
The bell was silent in the air
And all the room one glow because
Time was away and she was here.

❖❖❖

Air: 'The love of a woman'

Robert Creeley 1926–2005

THIS IS VERY much a poet's love, because the essence of the love seems to be the poem that is left to commemorate it. The poet sees the love of a woman as the opportunity to capture a more enduring experience by verbalizing it, creating happiness for both of them.

The love of a woman
is the possibility which
surrounds her as hair
her head, as the love of her

follows and describes
her. But what if
they die, then there is
still the aura

left, left sadly, but
hovers in the air, surely,
where this had taken place?
Then sing, of her, of whom

it will be said, he
sang of her, it was the
song he made which made her
happy, so she lived.

———— ❖❖❖ ————

Wedding

Alice Oswald b. 1966

THIS IS A glorious celebration of the hugeness of love, sweeping us from image to image with an exultant hilarity that encompasses the world. Beside this, Elizabeth Browning's famous 'How do I love thee? Let me count the ways' appears almost timid and one-sided. Oswald asks us to abandon ourselves, abandon logic, abandon the plodding limitations of life and enter into the illumination that is love.

From time to time our love is like a sail
and when the sail begins to alternate
from tack to tack, it's like a swallowtail
and when the swallow flies it's like a coat;
and if the coat is yours, it has a tear
like a wide mouth and when the mouth begins
to draw the wind, it's like a trumpeter
and when the trumpet blows, it blows like millions
and this, my love, when millions come and go
beyond the need of us, is like a trick;
and when the trick begins, it's like a toe
tiptoeing on a rope, which is like luck;
and when the luck begins, it's like a wedding,
which is like love, which is like everything.

———— ❖❖❖ ————

A Valediction: Forbidding Mourning

John Donne 1572–1631

Donne moves smoothly and powerfully through a succession of extraordinary images whose exquisite appositeness may become evident only upon scrutiny. All culminates in the one extended metaphor when he takes the conceit of the compass and turns it into a sublime image of human love. Here one sees what makes Donne so supreme a poet. I am aware of no more beautiful lines about what it means to love and be loved than those in the second-last stanza.

> As virtuous men passe mildly away,
> And whisper to their soules, to goe,
> Whilst some of their sad friends doe say,
> The breath goes now, and some say, no:
>
> So let us melt, and make no noise,
> No teare-floods, nor sigh-tempests move,
> T'were prophanation of our joyes
> To tell the layetie our love.
>
> Moving of th'earth brings harmes and feares,
> Men reckon what it did and meant,
> But trepidation of the spheares,
> Though greater farre, is innocent.
>
> Dull sublunary lovers love
> (Whose soule is sense) cannot admit
> Absence, because it doth remove
> Those things which elemented it.
>
> But we by a love, so much refin'd.
> That our selves know not what it is,
> Inter-assured of the mind,
> Care lesse, eyes, lips, and hands to misse.

Our two soules therefore, which are one,
Though I must goe, endure not yet
A breach, but an expansion,
Like gold to ayery thinnesse beate.

If they be two, they are two so
As stiffe twin compasses are two,
Thy soule the fixt foot, makes no show
To move, but doth, if the'other doe.

And though it in the center sit,
Yet when the other far doth rome,
It leanes, and hearkens after it,
And growes erect, as that comes home.

Such wilt thou be to mee, who must
Like th'other foot, obliquely runne;
Thy firmnes drawes my circle just,
And makes me end, where I begunne.

PRAYER

S INCE I SPEND seven hours a day praying, you would think I had at the tips of my fingers many poems celebrating this most fundamental of actions. Prayer is extraordinarily difficult to speak about, at least for me, for to begin with it is not really an action at all. It is God who does the praying within us and I find myself sinking into very deep waters when I attempt to explain this.

Poets, one might think, would explain it better, but since there are no concepts into which prayer can be confined, no definitions except the simplest, the skill of the poets takes them little further than my own unskilled fumblings. This little cluster of poems is about prayer and from them one can deduce something of its all-embracing importance, its giving to us a truth more real than we can encompass on our own. St John of the Cross, who is, as far as I know, the only canonized poet, tended to take images from the natural beauty of the Spanish countryside to create an atmosphere that might suggest the wonder of contact with God.

Do not tell me, dear Reader, that you are a cheerful atheist and have no sense whatever of the transcendent. Do you not look at the night sky? Have you not seen the ocean? When you love, when you gaze in wonder, when you know moments of pure happiness, it seems to me you are in contact with that mystery I would call God. If your contact is anonymous, so be it.

Perhaps all I can say here is that I am fond of all these poems and have confidence that when you read them you will have your own sense of the transcendent in some way magnified.

The Garden

Harry Clifton b. 1952

CLIFTON'S GARDEN is most beautifully and lovingly described. Yet it is not what is in the garden and how delightful it is that is important, but the fact that he has found 'a closed space' on which he can always 'depend'. The garden is obviously his own interior space, that personal area that not all are fortunate enough to find, but in which alone we can be wholly at rest.

It was a closed space. From the moment I saw it
I knew I could depend on it.
To hell with the endless weathers
Passing above, and the high apartments
Shadowing it. Down here
On the stone bench, of an autumn morning,
I felt for a moment, the heat of sun on my face
As it angled around the corner
Out of sight. My patch of sky
Went blue then, or grey,
And I went inside.
                But it was always there,
The garden. At its centre
A tree, a plum tree
As I discovered, when the bluish fruit
Appeared through the leaves in September,
Gave it core, and strength, and definition.
Yellow courgettes, and ripening tomatoes

Bound to their splints. And tough carnations
Half in love with the wire that fenced them in.
And the clay, of course, rich and black
After rain, or a dry brown bath
For thrushes and sparrows.
And day after day, the same man
Clearing weeds, or laying a path
According to some unspecified plan.

No need to mention where all this was.
I had travelled enough, by then,
To dispense with where. Sufficient to say
A horse's tail appeared, one day,
Above a gable, or a streak of cirrus –
Time and the future, far away.
Woodsmoke, the waft of cooking,
Brought me back to earth –
I was here, in the garden. An old woman
With green fingers, fed me generic names
Like Flower, or Tree,
As if nothing else mattered
But the garden, and having your own key.

St Kevin and the Blackbird

Seamus Heaney b. 1939

THIS POEM IS based on a legend: the blackbird laid its egg in the saint's outstretched hand as he prayed. But the legend so charmingly recalled is merely a pretext for meditating upon the power of prayer. It can draw us free from the constraints of the body, or rather, make the body itself into prayer.

And then there was St Kevin and the blackbird.
The saint is kneeling, arms stretched out, inside
His cell, but the cell is narrow, so

One turned-up palm is out the window, stiff
As a crossbeam, when a blackbird lands
And lays in it and settles down to nest.

Kevin feels the warm eggs, the small breast, the
    tucked
Neat head and claws and, finding himself linked
Into the network of eternal life,

Is moved to pity: now he must hold his hand
Like a branch out in the sun and rain for weeks
Until the young are hatched and fledged and
    flown.

*

And since the whole thing's imagined anyhow,
Imagine being Kevin. Which is he?
Self-forgetful or in agony all the time

From the neck on out down through his
       hurting forearms?
Are his fingers sleeping? Does he still feel his
       knees?
Or has the shut-eyed blank of underearth

Crept up through him? Is there distance in his
       head?
Alone and mirrored clear in love's deep river,
'To labour and not to seek reward,' he prays,

A prayer his body makes entirely
For he has forgotten self, forgotten bird,
And on the riverbank forgotten the river's
       name.

Long-legged Fly
W. B. Yeats 1865–1939

YEATS SETS before us the great general Caesar, the great beauty Helen of Troy, the great artist Michelangelo, and shares with us his conviction that all they represent arises from an inward silence. However greatly gifted, the human mind is dependent upon an inward stillness. The conscious mind is like the long-legged fly that skitters on the water's surface, while the subconscious mind runs still and deep like a stream beneath it.

That civilisation may not sink,
Its great battle lost,
Quiet the dog, tether the pony
To a distant post;
Our master Caesar is in the tent
Where the maps are spread,
His eyes fixed upon nothing,
A hand under his head.

Like a long-legged fly upon the stream
His mind moves upon silence.

That the topless towers be burnt
And men recall that face,
Move most gently if move you must
In this lonely place.

She thinks, part woman, three parts a child,
That nobody looks; her feet
Practise a tinker shuffle
Picked up on a street.

Like a long-legged fly upon the stream
Her mind moves upon silence.

That girls at puberty may find
The first Adam in their thought,
Shut the door of the Pope's chapel,
Keep those children out.
There on that scaffolding reclines
Michael Angelo.
With no more sound than the mice make
His hand moves to and fro.

Like a long-legged fly upon the stream
His mind moves upon silence.

Calling

John Fuller b. 1937

THIS IS A POEM – a difficult one at first sight – about a mysterious awareness that many people discover within the context of their lives. Fuller cannot spell out what it is and yet he is certain that it is something greater than ourselves. He even describes it as 'commanding' and suggests that our awareness of beauty and of responsibility comes from this almost unheard and indescribable 'something'. He does dare to refer to it as a 'voice', and yet it is a 'voice' in no human sense – a summons that we cannot control, or knit into a pattern that makes secular sense to us.

> There, don't you hear it too?
> Something is calling, although
> The day is blank and gray.
>
> The eye fastened on nothing,
> The ear undistracted
> And we with nothing to say.
>
> But still that sense of calling,
> Of something seeking attention
> Beyond our consciousness.

That voice in voiceless things
When they cease to be themselves,
Losing their choice and purpose,

Joining the indiscriminate
Otherness which surrounds us
At our own times of withdrawal.

It is then that the world calls us
As if to reinterpret
Or to reconfigure.

Whose is this voice? A god's?
Surely not. It seems
To be the voice of duty

That speaks of origins
And of relationships
Between things grown apart.

And I remember the muezzin
Singing every morning
Raptly, as if for himself.

Singing in the dark hour
At a distance, over all,
And yet outside our door.

His practised lilt spoke more
Of the puzzles of night than of
The determinations of morning

As though the light had still
To be charmed into being
And each day a reward.

The voice is much like his,
A commanding meditation
Rising from the blankness

Of a sleeping senselessness,
Thoughtful, improbable,
But stirring us to beauty.

And like his, the voice
Links us for a while
In its reiterations

Then ends abruptly, as if
Distracted by something else
Of no great importance.

Albi, 1297

D. Nurkse b. 1949

DEATH BY enclosure or immuring becomes a complete glory for the Albigensian who, as we read the poem, is slowly enduring martyrdom. If we pray, we are indestructible and the very nature of the death becomes a means of self-fulfilment.

Because I could not believe
God wills us to suffer
I was sealed up in the wall.
They left a gap in which my body
could curl like a foetus,
and a little sky, which they filled in
brick by brick, and perhaps
it troubled the masons
to be immuring a human being,
for they whistled loudly, sometimes
a trowel shook, mortar spilt,
and yet it was a tight course:

I knew better than to press against it.
When the dark closed in
I lay listening to my pulse
louder, louder, and the distant voices
singing – I knew better
than to try to guess the words
or listen for my name.

Then I was the wall itself,
everything the voices long for
and cannot have – the self,
the stone inside the stone.

———— ❖❖❖ ————

Prayer

John Burnside b. 1955

Burnside opens with the unusual plea to be given a little less. It takes the whole of this short poem to understand what he is praying for. He feels himself inadequate to respond to the extraordinary abundance of natural beauty. He cannot pay it due reverence, respect it as it deserves. Really to see what is there, the luminous rightness of the simplest things, like his hands and his desk light, is beyond our natural capacity – hence the role of prayer.

Give me a little less
with every dawn:
colour, a breath of wind,
the perfection of shadows,

till what I find, I find
because it's there.
Gold in the seams of my hands
and the desk light burning.

INDEX OF FIRST LINES

SOURCES AND
ACKNOWLEDGEMENTS

W. H. AUDEN: 'This Lunar Beauty', 'Lullaby' and 'Musée des Beaux Arts' from *Collected Shorter Poems 1927–1957* (Faber & Faber, 1969).

ELIZABETH BISHOP: 'One Art' from *The Complete Poems 1927–1979* (Farrar, Straus & Giroux, 1983), © 1979, 1983 by Alice Helen Methfessel.

THOMAS BLACKBURN: 'A Broken Image' from *Selected Poems*, edited by Julia Blackburn (Carcanet Press, 2001), reprinted by permission of the publisher.

JOSEPH BRODSKY: 'Nativity Poem', translated by Seamus Heaney, from *Nativity Poems: Bilingual Edition* by Joseph Brodsky (Farrar, Straus & Giroux, 2002).

JOHN BURNSIDE: 'Prayer', © John Burnside, published by permission of the author.

CHARLES CAUSLEY: 'Eden Rock' from *Collected Poems 1951–1997* (Macmillan, 1997), reprinted by permission of David Higham Associates.

C. P. CAVAFY: 'Waiting for the Barbarians', translated by Edmund Keeley and Philip Sherrard, from *Collected Poems* (Chatto & Windus, 1990), reprinted by permission of The Random House Group Ltd.

AMY CLAMPITT: 'Lindenbloom' from *The Kingfisher* (Faber & Faber, 1983).

HARRY CLIFTON: 'The Garden' from *London Review of Books*, Volume 25, Number 20 (October 2003), reprinted by permission of the author.

CAROLE COATES: 'Fanfaronade' from *The Goodbye Edition* (Shoestring Press, 2005), reprinted by permission of the author.

DAVID CONSTANTINE: 'Watching for Dolphins' from *Collected Poems* (Bloodaxe Books, 2004), reprinted by permission of the publisher.

ROBERT CRAWFORD: 'Advice', in *The Times Literary Supplement*, 2004, © Robert Crawford, reprinted by permission of the author.

ROBERT CREELEY: 'Air: The Love of a Woman' from *Love: Poems 1950–1960* (Scribners, 1962).

e. e. cummings 'in Just-' and 'anyone lived in a pretty how town' from *Complete Poems 1904–1962*, edited by George J. Firmage (Liveright, 1994), © 1991 by the Trustees for the E. E. Cummings Trust and George J. Firmage, reprinted by permission of W. W. Norton & Company.

EMILY DICKINSON: 'A bird came down the walk', 'Because I could not stop for Death' and 'Success is counted sweetest' from *The Poems of Emily Dickinson*, edited by Thomas H. Johnson, Cambridge, Massachusetts: The Belknap Press of Harvard University Press, copyright © 1951, 1955, 1979, 1983 by the President and Fellows of Harvard College, reprinted by permission of the publisher.

ROBERT FROST: 'Fire and Ice' from *The Poetry of Robert Frost*, edited by Edward Connery Lathem (Jonathan Cape, 1969), reprinted by permission of The Random House Group Ltd.

JOHN FULLER: 'Calling' from *Ghosts*: (Chatto & Windus, 2004), reprinted by permission of The Random House Group Ltd.

ROBERT GRAVES: 'Welsh Incident' from *Complete Poems In One Volume*, edited by Patrick Quinn (Carcanet Press, 2000), reprinted by permission of the publisher.

ALASDAIR GRAY: 'A Censor Complains' from *Old Negatives* (Jonathan Cape, 1989).

ROBERT HAYDEN: 'Those Winter Sundays' from *Collected Poems of Robert Hayden*, edited by Frederick Glaysher (Liveright, 1966), © 1966 by Robert Hayden, reprinted by permission of Liveright Publishing Corporation.

SEAMUS HEANEY: from 'Lightenings' in *Seeing Things* (Faber & Faber, 1991), and 'St Kevin and the Blackbird' and 'Castalian Spring' from *The Spirit Level* (Faber & Faber, 1996).

JOHN HOLLANDER: 'Fiddle-Faddle' from *The New Criterion*, Volume 23, Number 9 (May 2005).

SHERI HOSTETLER: 'Instructions' from *A Cappella: Mennonite Voices in Poetry* by Ann Hostetler (University of Iowa Press, 2003), reprinted by permission of the author.

A. E. HOUSMAN: 'Into my heart an air that kills' and 'Loveliest of trees, the cherry now' from *Collected Poems and Selected Prose* (Penguin Twentieth-Century Classics, 1989), reprinted by permission of The Society of Authors as the Literary Representative of the Estate of A. E. Housman.

JOSEPHINE JACOBSEN: 'Old Mr Forrester' first appeared in *The New Yorker* (21 and 30 April 2001), © 2001 Josephine Jacobsen, reprinted by permission of Elizabeth Spires on behalf of the author's literary executor, Erlend Jacobsen.

PHILIP LARKIN: 'Church Going' and 'An Arundel Tomb' from *Collected Poems* (Faber & Faber, 1990), © the Estate of Philip Larkin, 1988.

DENISE LEVERTOV: 'Clouds' from *Poems 1960–1967* (New Directions, 1983), reprinted by permission of Pollinger Limited and the Estate of Denise Levertov.

GABRIEL LEVIN: 'Jerome' from *The Times Literary Supplement* (2 April 2004), reprinted by permission of the author.

ROGER LIPSEY: 'We had tired of confusion', © Roger Lipsey, published by permission of the author.

MICHAEL LONGLEY: 'Swans Mating' from *Selected Poems* (Jonathan Cape, 1998), reprinted by permission of The Random House Group Ltd.

ROBERT LOWELL: 'Epilogue' from *Day by Day* (Faber & Faber, 1977).

ROGER McGOUGH: 'The Wrong Beds (after Baudelaire)' from *The Way Things Are* (Viking Penguin, 1999), © Roger McGough 1999, reprinted by permission of PFD (www.pfd.co.uk) on behalf of the author.

LOUIS MacNEICE: 'Snow' and 'Meeting Point' from *Collected Poems* (Faber & Faber, 1979), reprinted by permission of David Higham Associates.

GLYN MAXWELL: 'The Snow Village' from *The Nerve* (Picador, 2002), reprinted by permission of the author and Macmillan London Ltd.

CHRISTOPHER MIDDLETON: 'Disturbing the Tarantula' from *The Word Pavilion: New & Selected Poems* (Carcanet Press, 2001), reprinted by permission of the publisher.

MARIANNE MOORE: 'Silence' from *Selected Poems* (Faber & Faber, 1969).

D. NURKSE: 'Albi 1297' from *The Times Literary Supplement*, 24 June 2005, reprinted by permission of the author.

MARY OLIVER: 'Can You Imagine?' from *Long Life: Essays and Other Writings* (Perseus Books, 2005).

ALICE OSWALD: 'Mountains' and 'Wedding' from *The Thing in the Gap-Stone Stile* (Oxford University Press, 1996), and 'Walking Past a Rose this June Morning' from *Woods Etc.* (Faber & Faber, 2006), reprinted by permission of PFD on behalf of Alice Oswald.

DON PATERSON: 'Waking with Russell' from *Landing Light* (Faber & Faber, 2003).

ROBERT PINSKY: 'Door' from *First Things to Hand* (Sarabande Books, 2006), © 2006 by Robert Pinsky, reprinted by permission of Sarabande Books Inc., www.sarabandebooks.org.

195

RUTH PITTER: 'The Bridge' from *Collected Poems* (Enitharmon Press, 1996), reprinted by permission of the publisher.

SYLVIA PLATH: 'Among the Narcissi' from *Collected Poems* (Faber & Faber, 1981).

CARL RAKOSI: 'Confession, 1931' from *London Review of Books*, Volume 25, Number 21 (6 November 2003), © 2003 Carl Rakosi, reprinted by permission of Marilyn J. Kane.

RAINER MARIA RILKE: 'Archaic Torso of Apollo', translated by Martin Greenberg,' from *The New Criterion*, Volume 19 (March 2001).

CHARLES SIMIC: 'The Lights Are On Everywhere' from *The New York Review of Books*, Volume 52, Number 19 (December 2005).

LOUIS SIMPSON: 'Carentan O Carentan' from *The Owner of the House: New Collected Poems 1940– 2001* (BOA Editions, 2003), © 2003 by Louis Simpson, reprinted by permission of BOA Editions Ltd, www.boaeditions.org.

STEVIE SMITH: 'Tenuous and Precarious' from *The Collected Poems of Stevie Smith* (Penguin Modern Classics, 1985).

WALLACE STEVENS: 'A Clear Day and No Memories' from *The Collected Poems of Wallace Stevens* (Faber & Faber, 1984).

WISLAWA SZYMBORSKA: 'Utopia', translated by Stanislaw Baranczak and Clare Cavanagh, from *View with a Grain of Sand: Selected Poems* (Harcourt Brace & Company, 1993).

R. S. THOMAS: 'A Marriage' from *Collected Later Poems 1988–2000* (Bloodaxe Books, 2004), reprinted by permission of the publisher, and 'The Bright Field' and 'Via Negativa' from *Collected Poems 1945–1990* (Dent, 1993), reprinted by permission of The Orion Publishing Group.

ROWAN WILLIAMS: 'Feofan Grek: The Novgorod Frescoes' from *The Poems of Rowan Williams* (Perpetua Press, 2002).

W. B. YEATS: 'The Wild Swans at Coole', 'Sailing to Byzantium' and 'Long-legged Fly' from *Collected Poems* (Picador, 1990), reprinted by permission of A. P. Watt Ltd on behalf of Michael B. Yeats.

Every effort has been made to acknowledge all copyright holders prior to going to press, but in some cases this has not proved possible. Constable & Robinson therefore wish to thank all copyright holders who are included without acknowledgement, and apologize for any errors and omissions in the above list. If contacted, the publisher will be pleased to rectify these at the earliest opportunity.